HOW TO ESCAPE SINS

The Ways and Means to Refrain From The Disobedience of Allāh

Based on the words of

IMĀM IBN AL-QAYYIM

'Uddah as-Sābirīn wa Dhakhīrah ash-Shākirīn'

DR. `ABDUR-RAZZĀQ IBN `ABDUL-MUHSIN AL-BADR

First Edition: 1434H/March 2014CE

Translation: Abūl-Layth Qāsim Ibn Aggrey Mutiva
Reviewed and Edited: Ḥikmah Publications
Ḥikmah Publications
ISBN: 978-1-4951-0354-4

Address:
Ḥikmah Publications
P.O. Box 44121
Philadelphia, PA. 19144
hikmahpubs@gmail.com

فهرس

Table of Contents

Biography of Imām Ibn al-Qayyim (رَحِمَهُ ٱللَّهُ)[1]

His Name

This *Salafī* Imām became well-known with the title Ibn Qayyim al-Jawzīyah because his father was the principal of the school al-Jawzīyah in Damascus. As for his name, it is: Shams al-Din, Abū ʿAbdullāh, Muḥammad bin Abū Bakr bin Ayyūb al-Zarʿī (an ascription to Azraʿ which is in the south of Syria), then Dimashqī, Ḥanbalī.

Date of Birth

He was born on the 7th of Safar in the year 691H (1292 CE) and was raised in a house of knowledge and excellence and this offered him the chance to take knowledge from the senior scholars of his time, at a time when the various sciences (of knowledge) had flourished.

His Teachers

He studied under al-Shihāb al-Nābilisī, Abū Bakr bin ʿAbd al-Daayim, al-Qādī Taqī al-Dīn Sulaimān, ʿĪsaa al-Mutʿim, Fāṭimah Bint Jawhar, Abū Naṣr Muḥammad bin ʿImād al-Dīn al-Shairāzī, Ibn Maktūm, al-Bahaa' bin ʿAsākir, ʿAlaa al-Dīn al-Kindī, Muḥammad bin Abū al-Fatḥ Baʿlabkī, Ayyūb bin al-Kamāl and al-Qādī Badr al-Dīn bin Jamāʿah.

He took the knowledge of the laws of inheritance from Ismāʿīl bin Muḥammad and read the Arabic language to Abū al-Fatḥ Baʿlabkī and al-Majd al-Tūnisī. He studied fiqh with a group of scholars, amongst them Ismāʿīl bin Muḥammad al-Harrānī. He took Uṣūl (fundamental issues regarding creed etc.) from al-Safī al-Hindī. As for his greatest teacher and his Shaikh whom he accompanied for 17 years from the years of his life,

[1] This biography was compiled by the noble brother Amjad Rafīq.

and who left the greatest impact upon him, then that is the Imām, the Mujaddid, Taqī al-Dīn Ibn Taymīyah.

He (Ibn al-Qayyim) took the same methodology as him and traversed his path in waging war against the People of Innovations and Desires and those who deviated from the religion.

His Students

As for his own students, then they are many. Amongst them, his son ʿAbdullāh, Ibn Kathīr, the author of al-Bidāyah Wa al-Nihāyah', and the *Imām* and *Ḥāfiẓ*, ʿAbd al-Raḥmān bin Rajab al-Baghdādī, al-Ḥanbalī, the author of Ṭabaqāt al-Ḥanābilah, and also Shams al-Dīn Muḥammad bin ʿAbd al-Qādir al-Nābilisī.

Historical Perspective of His Era

Ibn al-Qayyim lived in a time in which there was strife and internal confusion and chaos, as well as an external threat which was menacing the Islamic state. For this reason, he used to order for the rejection of separation and disunity and holding fast to the Book of Allāh and the Sunnah of His Messenger (صَلَّى ٱللَّهُ عَلَيْهِ وَسَلَّمَ).

Amongst his goals was returning to the fountains of the original (and pure) religion and purifying it from the innovations and desires. So he called for the destruction of the *madhhab* of *taqlīd* (blind-following) and a return to the *madhhab* of the Salaf and traversing upon their way and methodology.

And because of this we see that he did not restrict himself to the Ḥanbalī *madhhab* and often he would take the opinion and view of one of the various *madhhabs* or perhaps he may have an opinion which conflicts the opinion of all the other *madhhabs*.

Therefore, his *madhhab* was *ijtihād* and the rejection of *taqlīd*. As a result of this he incurred great harm and was imprisoned along with his shaikh, Ibn

Taymīyah, in the same prison, but in isolation from him. He was not released from the prison until after the death of the shaikh.

He took to teaching and giving verdicts for a number of years and (all) the people, without exception, benefitted from him. The scholars also testified to his knowledge and piety. Ibn Ḥajr said about him: "He had a courageous heart, was vast in knowledge and was well acquainted with the differences (of opinion) and the *madhāhib* of the *Salaf*."

Shaikh al-Islām, Muḥammad bin ʿAlī al-Shawkānī said: "He restricted (himself) to the (most) authentic of evidences, and admired acting upon them. He did not depend upon opinion (*ra'ī*), would overcome (others) with the truth and would not be harsh with anyone with respect to it."

Ibn Kathīr said: "He was attached to occupying himself with knowledge, day and night. He would pray and recite the Qur'ān much and was of excellent character; he showed great affection and friendship. He would not be jealous or envious."

Ibn Kathīr also said: "I do not know, in this time of ours, anyone in the world who worships greater than him. He used to have a particular manner with respect to the prayer. He would lengthen it a great deal, would extend its bowing and prostrating. Many of his associates would censure him at times but he would never return and leave alone this (action of his), may Allāh have mercy upon him."

And Mullaa ʿAlī al-Qārī said: "And whoever investigates the book *Sharḥ Manāzil al-Sā'irīn* (i.e. Madārij al-Sālikīn), it will become plain and clear to him that both of them (meaning Ibn al-Qayyim and Ibn Taymīyah) were amongst the most senior from Ahl al-Sunnah Wa al-Jamā'ah and amongst the Awliyā (of Allāh) of this Ummah."

Al-Hāfidh al-Suyūṭī said: "And he became one of the senior scholars in *tafsīr* (exegesis), *ḥadīth, uṣūl, furū'* (subsidiary matters) and Arabic language."

He authored and compiled in the field of *fiqh, uṣūl, siyar* (biography), history and the sciences of ḥadīth. Alongside this, he was a linguist, well-acquainted with grammar, and a poet. He had written much poetry.

His Death

He passed on to the mercy of His Lord at the latter time of 'Ishā, on the night of Thursday, 13th of Rajab in the year 751H (1350 CE) and was buried at the foot of Mount Qāsiyūn by Damascus.

He left behind many written works, amongst the most famous of which are:

1. Shifaa al-'Alīl
2. Miftāḥ Dār al-Sa'ādah
3. Zād al-Ma'ād fī Hadyi Khair al-'Ibād
4. Hādī al-Arwāḥ ilaa Bilād il-Afrāh
5. Ighāthah al-Lahfān fī Ḥukm Ṭalāq al-Ghaḍbān
6. Al-Jawāb Kāfī liman Sa'ala 'An Dawaa al-Shāfī
7. Madārij al-Sālikīn fī Manāzil al-Sā'irīn
8. Tahdhīb Sunan Abū Dāwūd
9. Al-Sawā'iq al-Mursalah 'Ala al-Jahmiyyah wa al-Mu'aṭṭilah
10. Raf' Yadain fī al-Ṣalāh
11. Kitāb al-Kabā'ir
12. Ḥukm Tārik al-Ṣalāh
13. Al-Kalim al-Tayyib Wa al-'Amal al-Ṣāliḥ
14. Sharḥ Asmā al-Ḥusna
15. I'lām al-Muwaqqi'īn 'An Rabb al-'Ālamīn

May Allāh have mercy upon this great and notable *Imām*, benefit the world by him and elevate his position, rank after rank, in the Hereafter.

بِسْمِ ٱللَّهِ ٱلرَّحْمَٰنِ ٱلرَّحِيمِ

In the name of *Allāh*, the Most-Merciful, the Bestower of Mercy.

All praise is due to *Allāh* the Lord of the creation. I bear witness that there is nothing worthy of worship except for *Allāh* who is without partner or equal. And I bear witness that Muḥammad (صَلَّىٰ ٱللَّهُ عَلَيْهِ وَعَلَىٰ آلِهِ وَسَلَّمَ) is His servant and Messenger – may the peace and blessings be upon him, his family and all his companions.

O *Allāh*, aid us and do not aid others against us, grant us victory and do not grant others victory over us, and bestow upon us what might benefit us and do not plot against us. Guide us and make guidance easy for us and assist us against those who transgress against us. O *Allāh*, make us from those who are mindful [of You], thankful [to You], and those who cry out [to You] and are repentant, humble and obedient to You. O *Allāh*, accept our repentance, purify us of our misdeeds, and make our proof strong and convincing. Guide our hearts, correct our tongues, and remove the ill will from our hearts.

Then as to what follows:

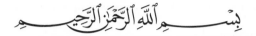

My noble brothers, in this gathering, the subject of our discussion will not be a clarification of the danger of sins and the magnitude of their harm upon the servant in his worldly life as well as his hereafter. This topic has been aptly addressed and discussed elaborately by *Imām* Ibn al-Qayyim (رَحِمَهُ ٱللَّهُ) in his monumental work '*Al-Jawāb al-Kāfī*'. Likewise, the discussion in this gathering will not revolve around repentance, nor its importance and its lofty station, nor the obligation of hastening to perform it and the dangers of delaying it or postponing it. It should be mentioned though that delaying repentance in itself is a sin that requires the servant to repent to *Allāh* (سُبْحَانَهُ وَتَعَالَىٰ). Instead, the topic of discussion for tonight's lecture will commence with the title that was advertised: "The ways and means to escape sins (*Al-Bawā'ith 'alá al-Khalāṣ min adh-Dhunūb*)."

The term '*al-bawā'ith*' refers to the things or the reasons that encourage the servant to repent and assist him to rush towards repentance and to avoid sins and remain far away from them, whenever a person's soul might incite them to commit a sin or an evil deed. This subject is very important to the extent that it should be studied and reflected upon. This is because an individual may find himself – and actually know his true condition – falling into some sins and performing acts of disobedience.

He may find within himself a desire to abandon these sins, but as time goes on he may continue to find himself falling into the same sins. So what are the inspirational factors that cause or assist the servant to avoid these sins, by the permission of *Allāh* (سُبْحَانَهُ وَتَعَالَى), stay far from them and ensure that the servant rushes to repent to *Allāh* (سُبْحَانَهُ وَتَعَالَى) whenever he has committed sins or fallen into them?

As you can see, this is an extremely important and incredibly significant subject. There are numerous things that assist the servant to escape sins, which have been discussed by the people of knowledge in their classical books, their beneficial works and valuable publications, which assist the servant - by the permission of *Allāh* (سُبْحَانَهُ وَتَعَالَى) - if he understood them and applied them in his life in order to escape sins and stay far away from them.

I found that the prominent *Imām* and celebrated educator Ibn al-Qayyim (رَحِمَهُ ٱللَّهُ) has extensively elaborated on this subject and provided invaluable benefit concerning it, as he often does in the majority of his books and written works. He mentioned (رَحِمَهُ ٱللَّهُ) this in his book '*'Uddah aṣ-Ṣābirīn wa Dhakhīrah ash-Shākirīn*' in a chapter which specifically deals with the things that help the servant to escape sins.

Ibn al-Qayyim (رَحِمَهُ ٱللَّهُ) mentioned twenty different motivational factors; he composed them in an amazing fashion, discussed them with succinctness and clarified them in a beneficial manner, in this chapter from the book that we have previously referred to.

In this gathering of ours, we will mention these things that *Imām* Ibn al-Qayyim (رَحِمَهُ ٱللَّهُ) has referred to in his book, which was previously cited, along with some further elaboration, asking *Allāh* (عَزَّوَجَلَّ) to bestow upon us His aid, success, and His guidance and that He does not leave us to our own selves for even the blinking of an eye. We ask Him to provide us with beneficial knowledge, to benefit us with what we have learned and to make what we have learned a proof for us and not a proof against us. And we ask Him to rectify all of our affairs and that he does not leave us to our own devices for even the blinking of an eye; surely He (تَبَارَكَ وَتَعَالَىٰ) is The All Hearing, The Always-Close (through his knowledge) and the One who answers.

1. Reverence and Veneration of Allāh[2]

The first of the ways to escape sins involves the reverence and veneration of *Allāh* (سُبْحَانَهُ وَتَعَالَىٰ). So the person acknowledges within his heart the exaltedness and magnificence of *Allāh* (سُبْحَانَهُ وَتَعَالَىٰ).

Allāh, the Exalted, said,

﴿ مَّا لَكُمْ لَا تَرْجُونَ لِلَّهِ وَقَارًا ﴿١٣﴾ وَقَدْ خَلَقَكُمْ أَطْوَارًا ﴿١٤﴾ ﴾

"What is [the matter] with you that you do not attribute to Allāh [due] magnificence? While He has created you in stages?" [*Sūrah Nūḥ* 71:13-14]

And He (عَزَّوَجَلَّ) said:

﴿ وَمَا قَدَرُوا۟ ٱللَّهَ حَقَّ قَدْرِهِۦ وَٱلْأَرْضُ جَمِيعًا قَبْضَتُهُۥ يَوْمَ ٱلْقِيَٰمَةِ وَٱلسَّمَٰوَٰتُ مَطْوِيَّٰتٌۢ بِيَمِينِهِۦ ۚ سُبْحَٰنَهُۥ وَتَعَٰلَىٰ عَمَّا يُشْرِكُونَ ﴿٦٧﴾ ﴾

"They made not a just estimate of *Allāh* such as is due to Him. And on the Day of Resurrection the whole of the earth will be grasped by His Hand and the heavens will be rolled up in His Right Hand. Glorified is He, and High is He above all that they associate as partners with Him." [*Sūrah az-Zumar* 39:67]

---

[2] **[PN]** The chapter headings have been added.

If a person's soul encourages them to commit a sin or act of disobedience, then they should acknowledge with their heart and attest to *Allāh*'s magnificence and greatness and they should also remember that their Magnificent and Venerated Lord is watching them, observing their actions and listening to their statements. Thus, if this preventative factor affects the heart it inhibits, deters and prevents the individual from committing sin, by the permission of *Allāh* (سُبْحَانَهُ وَتَعَالَىٰ).

2. The Love of Allāh

The second way to escape sins is for the heart to actualize the love of *Allāh* (سُبْحَانَهُ وَتَعَالَىٰ). There are various matters that have been mentioned by the people of knowledge that stimulate this love within the heart and enhance the strength of it in the heart of the servant.

So if a person's heart is driven by the love of *Allāh* (سُبْحَانَهُ وَتَعَالَىٰ), then this will keep him preoccupied and prevent him from falling into what angers *Allāh* (عَزَّوَجَلَّ). This is because true love causes an individual to stay away from whatever might be detestable to the one who he loves. For this reason it is said:

تعصي الإله وأنت تظهر حبه   هذا لعمري في القياس شنيعُ

لو كان حبك صادقًا لأطعته   إن المحب لمن أحب مطيعُ

"You disobey *Allāh* while making it appear that you love Him. This is despicable according to logic.

If your love were true, you would certainly obey him. Surely, the lover is obedient to the one who he loves."

3. Acknowledgment and Recognition of the Blessings of Allāh

The third way to escape sins is for the heart to acknowledge and recognize the blessings of *Allāh* and His benevolence towards His servant. He has favored His servant with health and wellbeing, wealth, a home and transportation, just as He has favored His servant with hearing, sight, and strength.

So the servant should remember the favor of *Allāh* (سُبْحَانَهُ وَتَعَالَى) upon him and be careful not to allow himself to be in a wretched state. Since the blessings of *Allāh* continue to be bestowed upon him, while the angels ascend with evil deeds, false statements and unlawful actions that he committed.

There is a story mentioned by some of the people of knowledge where a sinful man once approached a person of knowledge at a time when his soul was inciting him to commit sins. So the person of knowledge said to the man, "If you intend to sin then go to a place where *Allāh* cannot see you." The man responded by saying, "This is not possible." Then the scholar responded by saying, "Therefore, you should not use any of the blessings which *Allāh* has bestowed upon you to disobey Him." The man inquired, "How is that possible?" Then the scholar reminded him of two things: the blessing of *Allāh* upon him and the fact that *Allāh* (سُبْحَانَهُ وَتَعَالَى) is watching him. This is the meaning of the scholar's words.

There is no doubt that whenever the servant reflects over how *Allāh* has blessed him with health, wellbeing, wealth, and the like of this and that all of this is from the favors of *Allāh* (سُبْحَانَهُ وَتَعَالَى) upon him; and he remembers the dangers associated with these sins, then indeed his consideration of this blessing, favor and goodness is from the greatest of preventative factors that help the servant to stay far away from sins and committing them.

ည❋❋❋ႀ

4. Reflecting Over the Punishment of Allāh

The fourth way to escape sins is to be conscious of the anger and recompense of *Allāh*, since *Allāh* (سُبْحَانَهُ وَتَعَالَى) is angered by those who disobey Him and He is displeased with those who do things that He has prohibited.

﴿ فَلَمَّآ ءَاسَفُونَا ٱنتَقَمْنَا مِنْهُمْ فَأَغْرَقْنَٰهُمْ أَجْمَعِينَ ٥٥ ﴾

"So when they angered Us, We punished them, and drowned them all." [*Sūrah az-Zukhruf* 43:55]

So *Allāh* (عَزَّوَجَلَّ) becomes angry, displeased and punishes. This should be remembered whenever a person's soul incites him to disobey *Allāh* (سُبْحَانَهُ وَتَعَالَى).

He should know that the anger of *Allāh* and His punishment cannot be repelled by anything. So what about this weak servant?!

Therefore, being aware of the anger of *Allāh* (سُبْحَانَهُ وَتَعَالَى) is among the greatest deterrents, hindrances and obstacles to the servant committing sins.

༺❋❋❋༻

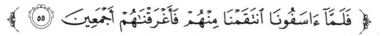

5. The Great Loss that Results From Sin

The fifth way to escape sins and disobedience is to be conscious of the loss this [results in]. Whenever an individual obeys their soul to commit a sin which it entices them towards, how much good do they lose out on? How much favor does he sacrifice? How much will this disobedience affect his level of faith as it relates to its completion and perfection? Consider the significance of this meaning and this loss in light of the statement of the Prophet (ﷺ):

« لاَ يَزْنِي الزَّانِي حِينَ يَزْنِي وَهُوَ مُؤْمِنٌ وَلاَ يَسْرِقُ السَّارِقُ حِينَ يَسْرِقُ وَهُوَ مُؤْمِنٌ وَلاَ يَشْرَبُ الْخَمْرَ حِينَ يَشْرَبُهَا وَهُوَ مُؤْمِنٌ »

> "The adulterer who commits adultery is not a believer[3] while he is committing adultery. And the thief who commits theft is not a believer while he is stealing. And the drunk who consumes intoxicants is not a believer while he is consuming intoxicants."[4]

So how much does an individual deprive himself of from favor and good and from deserving to be described as possessing complete faith? This is because on account of these acts of disobedience and major sins he does not deserve to be called anything but a disobedient believer, a transgressing believer, or a sinful believer or something similar to this from the titles that indicate that he committed these things.

Consequently, he deprives himself from an abundance of good. He loses out on his position and share of completeness of faith and its perfection,

---

[3] [PN] Shaykh al-Fawzān said, "The faith that has been negated here is the perfect and complete faith, and not the basis of faith itself." *al-Wāsiṭīyah*, p. 88.
[4] **[PN]** Bukhārī (no. 2475) and Muslim (no.57).

which is obligatory, in addition to everything that is related to it in terms of reward and goodness. How much does a person lose from what has been mentioned in the statement of *Allāh*?

﴿ مَنْ عَمِلَ صَٰلِحًا مِّن ذَكَرٍ أَوْ أُنثَىٰ وَهُوَ مُؤْمِنٌ فَلَنُحْيِيَنَّهُۥ حَيَوٰةً طَيِّبَةً ۖ وَلَنَجْزِيَنَّهُمْ أَجْرَهُم بِأَحْسَنِ مَا كَانُوا۟ يَعْمَلُونَ ﴿٩٧﴾ ﴾

> "Whoever works righteousness, whether male or female, while he is a true believer; verily to him We will give a good life, and We shall certainly pay them a reward in proportion to the best of what they used to do." [*Sūrah an-Naḥl* 16:97]

How many great things and lofty affairs has he deprived himself of in his worldly life and hereafter due to disobedience and sins? So if he is conscious of this and if he reminds himself whenever he is tempted with disobedience of how much he stands to lose by committing these sins and acts of obedience and how much good, favor, and blessings he is sacrificing in his worldly life as well as his hereafter; then there is no doubt that the soul being attentive with this type of consciousness, which is the perception of this loss, is extremely beneficial to avoid sins and stay far away from them.

6. Suppressing One's Soul And Conquering The Devil

The sixth way to escape sins involves suppressing one's desires and subduing the devil. The soul and the devil are the source of every sin and the origin of all evil. If he distanced himself from sinfulness and wrongdoing to which his soul that calls to evil and the accursed devil incites him, then he would have successfully suppressed his own soul and subdued the devil. In doing so he has tasted the sweetness of true strength through the obedience of *Allāh*, pursuing His pleasure and avoiding whatever He is displeased with. It has been narrated in the supplication which every Muslim is encouraged to say in the morning, in the evening and whenever he goes to bed,

« اللَّهُمَّ فَاطِرَ السَّمَوَاتِ وَالْأَرْضِ، عَالِمَ الْغَيْبِ وَالشَّهَادَةِ، رَبَّ كُلِّ شَيْءٍ وَمَلِيكَهُ، أَشْهَدُ أَنْ لَا إِلَهَ إِلَّا أَنْتَ، أَعُوذُ بِكَ مِنْ شَرِّ نَفْسِي، وَشَرِّ الشَّيْطَانِ وَشِرْكِهِ، وَأَنْ أَقْتَرِفَ عَلَى نَفْسِي سُوءًا أَوْ أَجُرَّهُ إِلَى مُسْلِمٍ »

"O *Allāh*, the Creator of the heavens and earth, the Knower of all things hidden and apparent, the Lord and Sovereign over all things; I bear witness that none has the right to be worshipped except You. I seek refuge with You from the evil of my own soul, from the evil of the devil and his *shirk* and from committing evil against my own soul or bringing it to another Muslim."[5]

[5] **[PN] Ṣaḥīḥ:** Collected by al-Tirmidhī and others. Declared *Ṣaḥīḥ* by Shaykh Albānī *Ṣaḥīḥ Sunan al-Tirmidhī* (no. 3529).

This is an example of seeking refuge [with Allāh] from the two sources of evil and their consequences. Surely the two sources of evil are the soul and the devil. Therefore, it is required of you in this blessed supplication to seek refuge with *Allāh* from the two sources of evil, which are the soul that incites to evil and the devil, three times: when you awake, when you enter the evening and when you retire to bed, from the two sources of evil.

It is also required of you to seek refuge with *Allāh* from the consequences of these things which is the perpetration of evil against yourself or to bring evil to someone else. If you are mindful of this and abandon disobedience, suppressing the soul that incites to evil, subduing your enemy the devil and seeking honor through obedience to *Allāh* (سُبْحَانَهُ وَتَعَالَى), then this is a treasure that is greater than any other.

❀***❀

7. The Compensation And Reward

The seventh way to escape sins is to be conscious of the reward and compensation. Whenever you abandon disobedience, which is actually part of your faith, out of the fear of *Allāh*, in pursuit of His pleasure, in an effort to safeguard your faith and seeking success through attainment of the pleasure of your Lord (سُبْحَانَهُ وَتَعَالَىٰ), then how much will *Allāh* compensate you for abandoning these things? Compensation is in the form of delight, happiness, and joy of the heart, felicity, blessings in this life and the other forms of good.

Whoever leaves something for *Allāh* will find that *Allāh* will replace it for him with that which is better. Thus, whenever one's soul incites them to commit a sin, then they should admonish it to abandon whatever it is inciting them towards, seeking compensation, which comprises of the vast amount of good of this worldly life and the hereafter, with which *Allāh* (سُبْحَانَهُ وَتَعَالَىٰ) honors His believing servant who abandons disobedience out of fear of his Lord, hope for His reward and in pursuit of the success that He has promised.

Abandoning sinfulness is obedience in itself, an act of devotion to *Allāh* (سُبْحَانَهُ وَتَعَالَىٰ) and a part of your faith through which you draw closer to *Allāh*. This understanding is established by several proofs and evidences, from them is the narration of *Abū Hurayrah* (رَضِيَ ٱللَّهُ عَنْهُ) which has been previously mentioned,

« لاَ يَزْنِي الزَّانِي حِينَ يَزْنِي وَهُوَ مُؤْمِنٌ ... »

"The adulterer who commits adultery is not a believer while he is committing adultery..."

8. The Ma'iyyah[6] of Allāh

The eighth way to escape sins is to be conscious of the *ma'iyyah* of *Allāh* (*al-ma'iyyah al-khāṣah*). I mean by this *Allāh's ma'iyyah* (سُبْحَانَهُ وَتَعَالَىٰ) that is specific to His patient and pious servants. So if one's soul incites them towards sinfulness, they are patient, fear *Allāh* (عَزَّوَجَلَّ) and afraid of His punishment. For this, the servant is rewarded with the specific *ma'iyyah* of *Allāh*, as *Allāh* said in His statement:

﴿ إِنَّ ٱللَّهَ مَعَ ٱلصَّـٰبِرِينَ ﴿١٥٣﴾ ﴾

"Truly *Allāh* is with the patient." [*Sūrah al-Baqarah* 2:153]

And *Allāh* (عَزَّوَجَلَّ) said:

﴿ إِنَّ ٱللَّهَ مَعَ ٱلَّذِينَ ٱتَّقَوا۟ وَّٱلَّذِينَ هُم مُّحْسِنُونَ ﴿١٢٨﴾ ﴾

"Truly *Allāh* is with those who fear Him, and those are good doers." [*Sūrah an-Naḥl* 16:128]

The *ma'iyyah* of *Allāh* in the specific sense necessitates victory, protection, assistance, aid, and success. The individual is mindful of this type of *ma'iyyah* and strives to become from those who deserve it. So he remains patient in abandoning disobedience that his own soul calls him to and he fears *Allāh* (سُبْحَانَهُ وَتَعَالَىٰ) by avoiding what *Allāh*, the Mighty and Majestic, is displeased with. Likewise he strives to perfect his worship of *Allāh* and his deeds in order to become from those who are deserving of this specific type of *Allāh's ma'iyyah* (*al-ma'iyyah al-khāṣah*).

---

6 **[PN]** The specific type of *ma'iyyah* is with respect to His help, assistance and protection, whereas the general type of *ma'iyyah* is with respect to the knowledge and awareness of *Allāh*.

9. The Imminent Approach of Death

The ninth way to escape sins, from the ways mentioned by Ibn al-Qayyim (رَحِمَهُ ٱللَّهُ), is to be attentive of the imminent approach of death. *Allāh* the (سُبْحَانَهُۥ وَتَعَالَىٰ) said,

﴿ لِكُلِّ أَجَلٖ كِتَابٞ ﴿٣٨﴾ ﴾

> "For each and every matter there is a decree." [*Sūrah ar-Ra'd* 13:38]

Man is oblivious to when death will suddenly come upon him and when his appointed time will arrive. Perhaps he thinks to himself, especially when he is strong and young, that he will live until well after his sixties, even though he may die tomorrow.

﴿ إِنَّ ٱللَّهَ عِندَهُۥ عِلۡمُ ٱلسَّاعَةِ وَيُنَزِّلُ ٱلۡغَيۡثَ وَيَعۡلَمُ مَا فِي ٱلۡأَرۡحَامِۖ وَمَا تَدۡرِي نَفۡسٞ مَّاذَا تَكۡسِبُ غَدٗاۖ وَمَا تَدۡرِي نَفۡسُۢ بِأَيِّ أَرۡضٖ تَمُوتُۚ إِنَّ ٱللَّهَ عَلِيمٌ خَبِيرُۢ ﴿٣٤﴾ ﴾

> "No person knows what he will earn tomorrow, and no person knows in what land he will die. Verily, Allāh is All-Knower, All-Aware (of things)." [*Sūrah Luqmān* 31:34]

So being conscious of the imminent approach of death and the fact that it can come upon the servant unexpectedly at any time is a significant cause for contemplation, if the servant reflected upon it. And the Prophet (صَلَّىٰ ٱللَّهُ عَلَيْهِ وَسَلَّمَ) said,

« أَكْثِرُوا ذِكْرَ هَاذِمِ اللَّذَّاتِ »

"Constantly remember the destroyer of pleasures."[7]

This deliberation will benefit the servant by helping him to avoid sins, stay far away from them and distance himself from them. If his soul incites him to go to such and such a place, regardless of whether it involves travel or not or is near or far, he can respond to his soul by saying,

" هبِ يا نفس أنك متِّ في الطريق أو متِّ في هذا السفر "

"O soul, suppose that you were to die on the way or during this trip."

This has really happened. A person left their land and travelled with the sole intention – and *Allāh's* refuge is sought – to commit sins during this trip and suddenly died in this state. Thinking about this type of situation, frightening oneself with it and reminding oneself that a person may die unexpectedly and leave this world while they were committing sins and pursuing acts of disobedience - and Allāh's refuge is sought.

This is an extremely dangerous matter and no intelligent person would wish for himself to die in this state or to pass away while he was on this path - and *Allāh*'s refuge is sought. This is an important reminder, if a person was to visualize and reflect upon it, then by the permission of *Allāh* (سُبْحَانَهُ وَتَعَالَى) it will become a protective barrier and prevent him from committing sin.

---

[7] **[PN] Ṣaḥīḥ**: Collected by Ibn Mājah. This hadith was declared *Ṣaḥīḥ* by Shaykh Albānī *Ṣaḥīḥ Sunan Ibn Mājah* (no. 3453).

10. Calamities Are A Consequence Of Sins

The tenth way to escape sins is to be conscious of the calamity [that results from sin] and the wellbeing [that results from obedience]. This is also a great point of reflection, which if a person acknowledges with his heart and reflects upon this with his mind then it will assist him to fight against his own soul, in order to remain far away from the disobedience of *Allāh* (سُبْحَانَهُ وَتَعَالَىٰ).

As it pertains to calamities and well-being, then sins represent the greatest of trials; and well-being is [coupled] to the obedience of *Allāh* (سُبْحَانَهُ وَتَعَالَىٰ). The people of obedience are those who are in a state of wellbeing while the people of sins are the people of calamities. So calamities are connected to sins and wellbeing is connected to the obedience of *Allāh* (سُبْحَانَهُ وَتَعَالَىٰ).

A person may be tested with something that affects his body but he is in the most complete state of wellbeing as it relates to his religion and the best state of well-being in his religion. Conversely, an individual may be in a state totally opposite to that where he is of sound body but he is not in a good state in terms of his religion.

Allāh has given the latter person strength, a sound body, health, and wealth yet he is not in a good state as it relates to his religion, as sins have destroyed and ruined him. So he should think about this since it contains great benefit for him - by the permission of *Allāh*.

11. Striving Against The Soul

The eleventh way to escape sins that *Ibn al-Qayyim* (رَحِمَهُ ٱللَّهُ) mentioned is to progressively become accustomed to countering the call to lusts and desires through religious motivation. This means that a person trains himself to strive against his soul, as *Allāh* (سُبْحَانَهُ وَتَعَالَى) said:

﴿ وَٱلَّذِينَ جَٰهَدُواْ فِينَا لَنَهْدِيَنَّهُمْ سُبُلَنَاۚ وَإِنَّ ٱللَّهَ لَمَعَ ٱلْمُحْسِنِينَ ٦٩ ﴾

> "As for those who strive hard for Us, We will surely guide them to Our Paths. And verily, *Allāh* is with the good doers." [*Sūrah al-ʿAnkabūt* 29:69]

Thus, the Muslim possesses religious motivation; rather, there are several religious motivational factors as we have previously mentioned, just as there are evil temptations and stimuli that come from here and there.

So he needs to treat, repel and struggle with the temptations that call him towards evil through the religious motivation, which is called (*mujāhadah*). *Mujāhadah* is a form of resistance (*muqāwamah*) that involves resisting the temptations that incite evil within his soul and call to it.

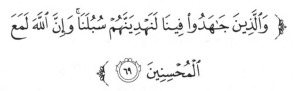

12. Repelling Evil Thoughts

The twelfth way to escape sins and disobedience, as mentioned by *Ibn al-Qayyim* (رَحِمَهُ ٱللَّهُ), is to repel evil thoughts from one's soul. This is because disobedience starts as a thought and develops into a desire.

Then it becomes an intention that grows within the heart of the servant. Then this intention changes into an evil will; then after this it develops into a determination that is linked to the action.

So it is best for a person to cut off these evil thoughts from the very beginning because if they are not eradicated from the very beginning they will increase and evolve from one thing into another, as we have mentioned.

It is easier for him to repel and conquer these thoughts and ideas while they are still merely thoughts existing in his mind, before they grow and evolve within his soul and become a strong intention or an evil will or determination to commit the sin and perpetrate it.

ꕤ ❋ ❋ ❋ ꕤ

13. Severing Any Relationships Or Causes That Stir Unlawful Desires

The thirteenth way of escaping sins as mentioned by *Ibn al-Qayyim* (رَحِمَهُ ٱللَّهُ) is to sever all connections and reasons that provoke him to follow his desires by redirecting his desires towards whatever is pleasing to *Allāh*.

This is because there are many different reasons that stir in a person's heart the desire for falsehood, sin and that which is unlawful. So the person must strive to sever these connections and reasons that rouse within his heart the call to sinfulness.

This is not achieved by completely eliminating his desires; rather, an individual should direct his desires to what pleases *Allāh*, as found in the *ḥadīth* that has been narrated by *Anas* (رَضِيَ ٱللَّهُ عَنْهُ),

« لَا يُؤْمِنُ أَحَدُكُمْ حَتَّى يَكُونَ هَوَاهُ تَبَعًا لِمَا جِئْتُ بِهِ »

> "None of you truly believes until his desires coincide with what I have brought."[1]

---

[1]**[PN] Ḍaʿīf:** Shaykh Albānī declared this ḥadīth to be *Ḍaʿīf* in his checking of *Sunnah Ibn Abū ʿĀṣim* (no. 15). Shaykh Ibn al-ʿUthaymīn said the meaning of this *ḥadīth* is sound.

14. Contemplating Upon The Legislated And Universal Signs Of Allāh

The fourteenth way to escape sins is to reflect upon the amazing recited signs of *Allāh* (سُبْحَانَهُ وَتَعَالَىٰ), which is His speech as found in the Noble *Qur'ān*. Similarly, to contemplate on the universal signs of *Allāh* as found within the creation of *Allāh* (سُبْحَانَهُ وَتَعَالَىٰ).

﴿ إِنَّ فِي خَلْقِ ٱلسَّمَٰوَٰتِ وَٱلْأَرْضِ وَٱخْتِلَٰفِ ٱلَّيْلِ
وَٱلنَّهَارِ لَءَايَٰتٍ لِّأُو۟لِى ٱلْأَلْبَٰبِ ﴿١٩٠﴾ ٱلَّذِينَ يَذْكُرُونَ ٱللَّهَ
قِيَٰمًا وَقُعُودًا وَعَلَىٰ جُنُوبِهِمْ وَيَتَفَكَّرُونَ فِى خَلْقِ
ٱلسَّمَٰوَٰتِ وَٱلْأَرْضِ رَبَّنَا مَا خَلَقْتَ هَٰذَا بَٰطِلًا سُبْحَٰنَكَ فَقِنَا
عَذَابَ ٱلنَّارِ ﴿١٩١﴾ ﴾

> "Verily, in the creation of the heavens and the earth, and the alternation of night and day, there are indeed signs for men of understanding. Those who remember *Allāh* standing, sitting, and lying down on their sides, and they think deeply about the creation of the heavens and the earth, [saying]: 'Our Lord, You have not created this without purpose. Glory to You! Give us salvation from the torment of the Fire." [*Sūrah Āl-'Imrān* 3:190-191]

Occupying the heart with this type of reflection will no doubt open up avenues for the servant to embrace good and remain far away from falsehood, distraction and misguidance. Consider this meaning in light of the statement of the men of understanding,

﴿ رَبَّنَا مَا خَلَقْتَ هَٰذَا بَٰطِلًا ﴾

"Our Lord, You have not created this without purpose."
[*Sūrah Āl-'Imrān* 3:191]

So this type of reflection and profound insight and outlook resulted in this strong faith.

﴿ رَبَّنَا مَا خَلَقْتَ هَٰذَا بَٰطِلًا ﴾

"Our Lord, You have not created this without purpose."
[*Sūrah Āl-'Imrān* 3:191]

This indicates that the servant's reflection upon the great signs of *Allāh* strengthens his faith, increases his connection with *Allāh* (سُبْحَانَهُ وَتَعَالَىٰ) and repels the ignoble whispers. This is also from the greatest of affairs that benefit the servant in this issue.

15. Recognizing The Reality Of This World

The fifteenth way of escaping sins as mentioned by *Ibn al-Qayyim* (رَحِمَهُ ٱللَّهُ) is to reflect on the reality of this world, how quickly it will end and how it is a place of trial and a source of delusion.

﴿ ٱعْلَمُوٓا۟ أَنَّمَا ٱلْحَيَوٰةُ ٱلدُّنْيَا لَعِبٌ وَلَهْوٌ وَزِينَةٌ وَتَفَاخُرٌۢ بَيْنَكُمْ وَتَكَاثُرٌ فِى ٱلْأَمْوَٰلِ وَٱلْأَوْلَـٰدِ كَمَثَلِ غَيْثٍ أَعْجَبَ ٱلْكُفَّارَ نَبَاتُهُۥ ثُمَّ يَهِيجُ فَتَرَىٰهُ مُصْفَرًّا ثُمَّ يَكُونُ حُطَـٰمًا ﴾

"Know that the life of this world is only play and amusement, pomp and mutual boasting among you, and rivalry in respect of wealth and children, as the likeness of vegetation after rain, thereof the growth is pleasing to the tiller; afterwards it dries up and you see it turning yellow; then it becomes straw." [*Sūrah al-Ḥadīd* 57:20]

There are numerous verses in the *Qur'ān* that clarify the reality of the life of this world. The same can be found in the narrations of the noble Messenger (صَلَّى ٱللَّهُ عَلَيْهِ وَسَلَّمَ). And *Allāh* says,

﴿ وَمَا ٱلْحَيَوٰةُ ٱلدُّنْيَآ إِلَّا مَتَـٰعُ ٱلْغُرُورِ ٢٠ ﴾

"And what is the worldly life except the enjoyment of delusion." [*Sūrah al-Ḥadīd* 57:20]

This means that the enjoyment is fleeting and temporary. He must think about how quickly this world ends, how quickly it will be over and how the real life is that of the hereafter, as *Allāh* said,

﴿ وَإِنَّ ٱلدَّارَ ٱلْآخِرَةَ لَهِىَ ٱلْحَيَوَانُ ﴾

> "And indeed, the home of the Hereafter - that is the [eternal] life." [*Sūrah al-ʿAnkabūt* 29:64]

As for the life of this world, then it is quickly over and will quickly disappear. Reflect upon this and the day when people will be made to stand before *Allāh* (سُبْحَانَهُ وَتَعَالَىٰ) on the Day of Judgment, when they await their reckoning. How long will they wait?

﴿ فِى يَوْمٍ كَانَ مِقْدَارُهُۥ خَمْسِينَ أَلْفَ سَنَةٍ ﴾

> "A Day the extent of which is fifty thousand years." [*Sūrah al-Maʿārij* 70:4]

What is the period that people spend in the life of this world compared to fifty thousand years? What is the lifespan of a person?

« أَعْمَارُ أُمَّتِي مَا بَيْنَ السِّتِّينَ إِلَى السَّبْعِينَ »

> "The life span of people from my nation is between sixty and seventy."[1]

If we suppose that a person lives for sixty years. If fifteen years, or a bit less, was subtracted from this, taking into account the period prior to puberty. Or suppose an entire third was subtracted from this due to sleep, because

[1] **[PN] Ḥasan**: Collected by *Imām* al-Tirmidhī in his Sunan. Shaykh Albānī declared this *ḥadīth* to be *ḥasan* in *Ṣaḥīḥ Sunan al-Tirmidhī* (no. 3550).

whoever lives sixty years and sleeps eight hours a night during this time will sleep for approximately twenty years.

Therefore, the time that you really utilize is your life is relatively small. What is this small amount of years compared to a day the extent of which is fifty thousand years? If the servant reflects upon how quickly this world passes by and how quickly it ends, then this will also be a great incentive for him to stay far from sin. Consider this meaning in light of the statement of the Prophet (ﷺ),

« كُنْ فِي الدُّنْيَا كَأَنَّكَ غَرِيبٌ أَوْ عَابِرُ سَبِيلٍ »

"Be in this world as though you are a stranger or a wayfarer."[1]

[1] **[PN]** Bukhari (no. 6416).

16. To Turn To Allāh

The sixteenth way to escape sins as mentioned by *Ibn al-Qayyim* (رَحِمَهُ ٱللَّهُ) is for the servant to turn to the One who the hearts of the servants are between His two fingers, the One in whose hands are all important matters and the One who controls and disposes of the servant's affairs. [Imagine the effects this will have] when the hearts turn to One who is in control of all of these things, rely upon Him and cling to Him (سُبْحَانَهُ وَتَعَالَىٰ).

﴿ وَمَن يَعْتَصِم بِٱللَّهِ فَقَدْ هُدِىَ إِلَىٰ صِرَٰطٍ مُّسْتَقِيمٍ ١٠١ ﴾

"And whoever holds firmly to *Allāh*, then he is indeed guided to a straight path." [*Sūrah Āl ʿImrān* 3:101]

And you ask Him to aid, protect, safeguard and look after you. There are numerous supplications that highlight this point, which have been authentically conveyed from the Prophet (صَلَّى ٱللَّهُ عَلَيْهِ وَسَلَّمَ). Whoever successfully supplicates to *Allāh* and places their trust and reliance in Him, will have their supplication accepted. *Allāh* (سُبْحَانَهُ وَتَعَالَىٰ) said,

﴿ وَقَالَ رَبُّكُمُ ٱدْعُونِىٓ أَسْتَجِبْ لَكُمْ ۚ إِنَّ ٱلَّذِينَ يَسْتَكْبِرُونَ
عَنْ عِبَادَتِى سَيَدْخُلُونَ جَهَنَّمَ دَاخِرِينَ ٦٠ ﴾

"And your Lord says: Call upon Me; I will answer you. Indeed those who are too proud to worship Me will enter the Hellfire in disgrace" [*Sūrah Ghāfir* 40:60]

And He (سُبْحَانَهُ وَتَعَالَىٰ) said,

﴿ وَإِذَا سَأَلَكَ عِبَادِى عَنِّى فَإِنِّى قَرِيبٌ أُجِيبُ دَعْوَةَ ٱلدَّاعِ إِذَا دَعَانِ ﴾

> "And when My servants ask you, concerning Me - indeed I am near. I respond to the invocation of the supplicant when he calls upon Me." [*Sūrah al-Baqarah* 2:186]

For this reason, it has been legislated for you to say whenever you leave your home,

« اللَّهُمَّ أَعُوذُ بِكَ أَنْ أَضِلَّ أَوْ أُضَلَّ أَوْ أَزِلَّ أَوْ أُزَلَّ أَوْ أَظْلِمَ أَوْ أُظْلَمَ أَوْ أَجْهَلَ أَوْ يُجْهَلَ عَلَيَّ »

> "O *Allāh*, I seek refuge in You lest I should stray or be led astray, or fall into error or be led to error, or to commit oppression or to be oppressed, or to behave ignorantly or to be treated ignorantly."[1]

This matter is extremely significant and whoever is granted success in this affair and is truthful in his reliance upon *Allāh* (سُبْحَانَهُ وَتَعَالَىٰ) will be protected, granted refuge and safeguarded. If an individual says, as found in the prophetic ḥadīth,

[1] **[PN] Ṣaḥīḥ**: Collected by *Imām* Abū Dāwūd in his *Sunan*. Shaykh Albānī declared it to be *Ṣaḥīḥ* in *Ṣaḥīḥ Sunan Abū Dāwūd* (no. 5094).

« إِذَا خَرَجَ الرَّجُلُ مِنْ بَيْتِهِ فَقَالَ بِسْمِ اللَّهِ تَوَكَّلْتُ عَلَى اللَّهِ، لَا حَوْلَ وَلَا قُوَّةَ إِلَّا بِاللَّهِ، يُقَالُ حِينَئِذٍ: هُدِيتَ، وَكُفِيتَ، وَوُقِيتَ، فَتَتَنَحَّى لَهُ الشَّيَاطِينُ فَيَقُولُ لَهُ شَيْطَانٌ آخَرُ: كَيْفَ لَكَ بِرَجُلٍ قَدْ هُدِيَ وَكُفِيَ وَوُقِيَ؟»

"When a man leaves his house, and says: 'In the Name of *Allāh*, I rely upon *Allāh*, there is no power and no might except with *Allāh*.' Then it is said: 'You have been guided, sufficed and protected.' Then the devils withdraw from him. Then another one of the devils says to him: 'What can you do to a man who has been guided, sufficed and protected?'"[1]

This demonstrates for us the lofty station and significant role of the legislated Islamic supplications and the authentic invocations, and the consequences of sincere reliance upon *Allāh* (سُبْحَانَهُ وَتَعَالَىٰ) in this important matter, which is the prevention of sins and avoiding them.

❀❀❀

[1] **[PN] Ṣaḥīḥ**: Collected by Abū Dāwūd in his *Sunan*. Shaykh Albānī declared it to be *Ṣaḥīḥ* in *Ṣaḥīḥ Sunan Abū Dāwūd* (no. 5095).

17. To Understand The Influence Of The Two Opposing Forces

The seventeenth way to escape sins is for the servant to know that he is influenced by two opposing forces. One force pulls him towards the Loftiest Companion (*Ar-Rafīq Al-A'lā*) and the other force pulls him towards the lowest of the low – and *Allāh*'s refuge is sought.

These two forces compete with one another to exert their influence on him. One force pulls him towards the Loftiest Companion (*Ar-Rafīq Al-A'lā*) through obedience since obedience raises the station of the servant, increases his standing and advances his rank.

﴿ يَرْفَعِ ٱللَّهُ ٱلَّذِينَ ءَامَنُوا۟ مِنكُمْ وَٱلَّذِينَ أُوتُوا۟ ٱلْعِلْمَ دَرَجَـٰتٍ ۚ

وَٱللَّهُ بِمَا تَعْمَلُونَ خَبِيرٌ ﴿١١﴾ ﴾

"*Allāh* will raise those who have believed among you and those who were given knowledge, in degrees." [*Sūrah al-Mujādilah* 58:11]

And He said,

﴿ إِلَيْهِ يَصْعَدُ ٱلْكَلِمُ ٱلطَّيِّبُ وَٱلْعَمَلُ ٱلصَّـٰلِحُ يَرْفَعُهُۥ ﴾

"To Him the good words raise and the righteous actions carry them." [*Sūrah Fāṭir* 35:10]

The other force pulls him towards the lowest of the low, and this is the force of the soul that incites him to evil, the devil, evil companions and corrupt associates. If an individual is moved by the forces of good he will be happy, prosperous, and safe and successful.

However, if an individual is moved by the forces of evil, he will be destroyed - and *Allāh*'s refuge is sought. This is another perspective that if the servant was to reflect upon and consider how he is pulled by two opposing forces, then he might scrutinize the advocates of evil and remind himself that this is what draws him towards the lowest of low. And as a result, he distances himself from traversing a path that will debase him or place him in a lowly state - and *Allāh*'s refuge is sought.

18. For Growth The Area Has To Be Clean And Empty

The eighteenth way to escape sins is to know that it is a condition for a place to be clear and empty in order for the rain of mercy to descend upon it; and it is a prerequisite for the place to be cleansed of filth for the vegetation to grow perfectly. When this occurs, and the place is clear and pure, it becomes ready and prepared for mercy, goodness and blessings.

Take the example that *Ibn al-Qayyim* (رَحِمَهُ ٱللَّهُ) alluded to regarding the condition of the vegetation. If the individual does not take it upon himself to remove the weeds and harmful plants that surround the vegetation and compete for its water, it is possible that they may consume more water than the trees; it is possible that these plants are harmful and it is possible there are insects that affect these trees by eating away at them and causing them to die or to become sick.

So this vegetation needs for the area to be purified in order to thrive and flourish in the best manner, just as it needs to be cleansed of weeds, strange plants and whatever else might harm it or consume [its nutrients]. As a result of this [care and treatment], if it is given ample water, then the water will have a significant effect upon its life, fruit, growth and strength.

Similarly, the believer is like the tree as mentioned in the Noble *Qur'ān*,

﴿ أَلَمْ تَرَ كَيْفَ ضَرَبَ ٱللَّهُ مَثَلًا كَلِمَةً طَيِّبَةً كَشَجَرَةٍ
طَيِّبَةٍ أَصْلُهَا ثَابِتٌ وَفَرْعُهَا فِى ٱلسَّمَآءِ ﴿٢٤﴾ تُؤْتِىٓ
أُكُلَهَا كُلَّ حِينٍۭ بِإِذْنِ رَبِّهَا ۗ وَيَضْرِبُ ٱللَّهُ ٱلْأَمْثَالَ
لِلنَّاسِ لَعَلَّهُمْ يَتَذَكَّرُونَ ﴿٢٥﴾ ﴾

> "Have you not considered how *Allāh* presents an example, [making] a good word like a good tree, whose root is firmly fixed and its branches [high] in the sky? It produces its fruit all the time, by permission of its Lord. And *Allāh* presents examples for the people that perhaps they will be reminded." [*Sūrah Ibrāhīm* 14:24-25]

Meaning that this is a similitude that is visible and noticeable: it is the example of the trees, which helps us to understand the reality of true faith. And the example of true faith is the example of a tree.

ꕥ❋❋❋ꕥ

19. Remember The Eternal Bliss Of Paradise

The nineteenth way of escaping sins as mentioned by *Ibn al-Qayyim* (رَحِمَهُ ٱللَّهُ) is for the servant to know that *Allāh* (سُبْحَانَهُ وَتَعَالَىٰ) has created him for an eternal existence which has no end, for honor and not humiliation, for tranquility and not fear, and for riches and not poverty. This is in the hereafter,

﴿ وَلَا خَوْفٌ عَلَيْهِمْ وَلَا هُمْ يَحْزَنُونَ ﴿١١٢﴾ ﴾

> "On such shall be no fear, nor shall they grieve." [*Sūrah al-Baqarah* 2:112]

Allāh (سُبْحَانَهُ وَتَعَالَىٰ) has created him for that. However, He tests him in this world with things and scenarios that are likely to distract him, or many of the people, and distract him regarding the reality of true life, honor, affluence, real enjoyment and other than that from the blessings of the hereafter which are unchanging and everlasting.

So reminding oneself of this and what exists in the afterlife from honor, affluence, enjoyment, blessings, safety and other than this, and that these sins will detrimentally affect his ability to acquire those lofty and higher stations, should cause him to strive hard to fight and combat against his own soul. So that he can succeed in acquiring the full enjoyment, bliss, tranquility and goodness of the hereafter and its blessings. Sins have a definite impact upon the servant on the day when he meets *Allāh* (سُبْحَانَهُ وَتَعَالَىٰ).

This is in opposition to the servant whom *Allāh* (سُبْحَانَهُ وَتَعَالَىٰ) has honored by protecting his faith and allowing him to pursue the pleasure of *Allāh* such that he becomes from the people of Paradise who enter it on the Day of

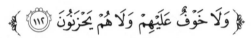

Judgment without any reckoning or punishment. As for anyone else [who doesn't fit this description], then they are subject to the reckoning and susceptible to the punishment of *Allāh* and entering the Hellfire.

If he was from the people of true faith but entered into the Hellfire, he will not remain in the Hellfire forever. This is because eternity in the Hellfire forever is specifically for the disbelievers. But the person of true faith by way of his own disobedience and sins places himself in serious danger and subjects himself to the like of this while in his grave, during his resurrection and on the day when he meets his Lord (سُبْحَانَهُ وَتَعَالَىٰ).

20. Knowledge Has To Be Accompanied By Action

The twentieth way to escape sins, which *Ibn al-Qayyim* (رَحِمَهُ ٱللَّهُ) concluded these motivational factors with, is for the servant to not be deluded by his belief that mere knowledge of what has been mentioned is sufficient enough to produce the desired results. So mere knowledge of the motivational factors for escaping sins that were mentioned by *Ibn al-Qayyim* (رَحِمَهُ ٱللَّهُ) is insufficient.

Rather, it is mandatory for this knowledge to be accompanied by the struggle against one's soul in order to act upon these matters. This advice from him (رَحِمَهُ ٱللَّهُ) is of the utmost importance. And these motivational factors for escaping sins are not just theoretical knowledge that is reviewed in circles of learning.

However, these are matters that must be carefully considered when faced with these situations in order to practically struggle against one's soul, in order to ensure its safety and well-being through staying away from sins and protecting oneself from them.

This is a summary of what *Ibn al-Qayyim* (رَحِمَهُ ٱللَّهُ) mentioned with the addition of some benefits, explanation and clarification. I advise everyone to review this beneficial chapter in the book '*'Uddah aṣ-Ṣābirīn wa Dhakhīrah ash-Shākirīn*' by *Imām Ibn al-Qayyim* (رَحِمَهُ ٱللَّهُ).

I have summarized his speech into approximately two and a half pages, which I will give to the brothers and, although it isn't perfect, I have done it so that this can be shared [via the various mediums] or so that it may be spread - by the will of *Allāh* - and perhaps benefit those who attended, as well as other than them by way of whatever means are available.

We ask *Allāh* the Most Generous, the Lord of the Magnificent throne by His greatest names and lofty attributes, because He is *Allāh* besides whom there is nothing deserving of worship besides Him, to benefit us all with what we have learned, that He increase us in knowledge, and rectify all of our affairs. [And I ask] that He does not leave us to our own devices for even the blinking of an eye. Surely He, the Blessed and Exalted, hears the supplication and with Him lies our hope. He is sufficient for us and a blessed maintainer of affairs.

And may the prayers of peace and blessings of *Allāh* be upon His servant and Messenger *Muḥammad*, his family and companions altogether.

The Actual Words of Imām Ibn al-Qayyim

فصل

وأما تقوية باعث الدين، فإنه يكون بأمور:

أحدها: إجلال الله تبارك وتعالى أن يعصى وهو يرى ويسمع، ومن قام بقلبه مشهد إجلاله لم يطاوعه قلبه لذلك ألبتة.

الثاني: مشهد محبته سبحانه، فيترك معصيته محبة له، فـ «إن المحب لمن يحب مطيع»[١]، وأفضل الترك ترك المحبين، كما أن أفضل الطاعة طاعة المحبين، فبين ترك المحب وطاعته وترك من يخاف العذاب وطاعته[٢]، بونٌ بعيد.

الثالث: مشهد النعمة والإحسان، فإن الكريم لا يعاملُ[٣] بالإساءة من أحسن إليه، وإنما يفعل هذا لئام الناس، فليمنعه مشهد إحسان الله ونعمته عن معصيته حياءً منه أن يكون خير الله وإنعامه نازلاً إليه[٤]، ومخالفاته ومعاصيه وقبائحه صاعدة إلى ربه، فمَلَكٌ ينزل بهذا وملكٌ يعرُج بهذا، فأقبِح بها من مقابلة! [٢٣/ ب].

الرابع: مشهد الغضب والانتقام، فإن الرب تعالى إذا تمادى العبد

---

(١) هذا عجز بيت منسوب لابن المبارك، وصدره: (لو كان حبك صادقًا لأطعته).
انظر: «تاريخ دمشق» (٣٢/ ٤٦٩) و «إحياء علوم الدين» (٤/ ٢٨١).
وهو منسوب أيضًا لمحمود الوراق.
انظر: «فوات الوفيات» (٤/ ٨١)، و «الكامل للمبرد» (٢/ ٤)، و «التمثيل والمحاضرة» ص (١٢).

(٢) ساقطة من الأصل، واستدركتها من النسخ الأخرى.

(٣) في النسخ الثلاث الأخرى: «يقابل».

(٤) في (م) و (ن): «عليه».

١٠٢

في معصيته غضب، وإذا غضب لم يقم لغضبه شيء، فضلاً عن هذا العبد الضعيف.

الخامس: مشهد الفوات، وهو ما يفوته بالمعصية من خير الدنيا والآخرة، وما يحدث له بها من كل اسم مذموم عقلاً وشرعًا وعرفًا، وتزول عنه من الأسماء الممدوحة شرعًا وعقلاً وعرفًا. ويكفي في هذا المشهد مشهد فوات الإيمان الذي أدنى مثقال ذرة منه خير من الدنيا وما فيها أضعافًا مضاعفة، فكيف يبيعه بشهوة تذهب لذتُها وتبقى سوء معيشتها[1]؟! تذهب الشهوة وتبقى الشقوة. وقد صح عن النبي ﷺ أنه قال: «**لا يزني الزاني حين يزني وهو مؤمن**»[2].

قال بعض الصحابة: «يُنزع منه الإيمان حتى يبقى على رأسه مثل الظُلّة؛ فإن تاب عاد إليه»[3].

وقال بعض التابعين: «يُنزع عنه الإيمان كما يُنزع عنه القميص فإن

(١) في (م) و (ن): «تبعتها» مكان: «سوء معيشتها»، وفي (ب): «تبعاتها».

(٢) رواه البخاري في «صحيحه» رقم (٢٤٧٥)، ومسلم في «صحيحه» رقم (٥٧)، كلاهما من حديث أبي هريرة رضي الله عنه.

(٣) انظر معناه عن الصحابة في: «شعب الإيمان» للبيهقي رقم (٥٣٦٧)، و «الشريعة» للآجري ص ١١٤ ـ ١١٥، و «شرح الاعتقاد للالكائي» رقم (١٨٦٩ ـ ١٨٧١، ١٨٧٧)، و «السنة» لعبدالله بن أحمد (١/ ٣٥١)، و «السنة» للخلال (٤/ ١٠٠، ١٠٢ ـ ١٠٣)، و «تعظيم قدر الصلاة» رقم (٥٣٨ ـ ٥٣٩).

وقد رواه أبو داود في «سننه» رقم (٤٦٩٠) عن أبي هريرة مرفوعًا، وصححه الحاكم في المستدرك (١/ ٢٢) علي شرط البخاري ومسلم، ووافقه الذهبي.

١٠٣

تاب لِبسه»[١].

ولهذا رأى النبي ﷺ في الحديث الذي رواه البخاري في صحيحه[٢] الزناة في التنور عراة؛ لأنهم تعرَّوا من لباس الإيمان، وعاد تنور الشهوة الذي كان في قلوبهم تنورًا ظاهرًا يحمى عليه بالنار.

السادس: مشهد القهر والظفر، فإن قهر الشهوة والظفر بالشيطان له حلاوة ومسرّة وفرحة عند من ذاق ذلك أعظم من الظفر بعدوّك من الآدميين وأحلى موقعًا وأتم فرحة. وأما عاقبته فأحمد عاقبة، وهو كعاقبة شرب الدواء النافع الذي أزال داء الجسد، وأعاده إلى صحته واعتداله.

السابع: مشهد العِوَض، وهو ما وعَد الله سبحانه به تعويض من ترك المحارم لأجله، ونهى نفسه عن هواها، وليوازن بين العوض والمعوض، فأيُّهما كان أولى بالإيثار اختاره وارتضاه لنفسه.

الثامن: مشهد المعيّة، وهي نوعان: معية عامة، ومعية خاصة. فالعامة اطلاع الرب تعالى عليه، وكونه بعينه لا تخفى عليه حاله، وقد تقدم.

والمقصود هنا: المعية الخاصة، كقوله: ﴿إِنَّ ٱللَّهَ مَعَ

---

(١) هو مروي عن خالد بن معدان. انظر: «الثقات» لابن حبان (٧/ ٤٢).
وقد جاء ذلك في حديث مرفوع إلى النبي ﷺ رواه الحاكم في «المستدرك» (١/ ٢٢) من حديث أبي هريرة رضي الله عنه.
وضعفه الألباني في «سلسلة الأحاديث الضعيفة» برقم (١٢٧٤).

(٢) صحيح البخاري رقم (١٣٨٦) من حديث سمرة بن جندب رضي الله عنه.

١٠٤

﴿ٱلصَّـٰبِرِينَ ۝٤٦﴾ [الأنفال: ٤٦]، وقوله: ﴿إِنَّ ٱللَّهَ مَعَ ٱلَّذِينَ ٱتَّقَوا۟ وَّٱلَّذِينَ هُم مُّحْسِنُونَ ۝١٢٨﴾ [النحل: ١٢٨]، وقوله: ﴿وَإِنَّ ٱللَّهَ لَمَعَ ٱلْمُحْسِنِينَ ۝٦٩﴾ [العنكبوت: ٦٩]، فهذه المعية الخاصة خير له وأنفع في دنياه وآخرته من قضاء [٢٤/ أ] وطره ونيل شهوتِه على التمام من أول العمر إلى آخره، فكيف يؤثر عليها لذة مُنغّصة مُنكّدة في مدة يسيرة من العمر، إنما هي كأحلام النائم أو ظل زائل؟!

التاسع: مشهدُ المغافصة[١] والمعاجلة[٢]، وهو: أن يخاف[٣] أن يغافصَه الأجلُ؛ فيأخذه الله عز وجل على غِرّة، فيحال بينه وبين ما يشتهي من لذات الدنيا وبينه وبين ما يشتهي من لذات الآخرة، فيا لها من حسرة ما أمرّها وما أصعبها، [لكن ما يعرفها إلا من جربها][٤]!

وفي بعض الكتب القديمة: «يا من لا يأمن على نفسه طرفة عين ولا يتم له سرور يوم، الحذر الحذر»[٥].

العاشر: مشهد البلاء والعافية، فإن البلاء في الحقيقة ليس إلا الذنوب وعواقبها، والعافية المطلقة هي الطاعات وعواقبها؛ فأهل البلاء هم أهل المعصية وإن عوفيت أبدانهم، وأهل العافية هم أهل الطاعة وإن

---

(١) غافص الرجل مغافصة وغفاصًا: أخذه على غرّة. «لسان العرب» (٧/ ٦١).

(٢) في (ب): «والمعالجة». وهو خطأ.

(٣) جملة «أن يخاف» ساقطة من الأصل، واستدركتها من النسخ الأخرى.

(٤) ما بين المعقوفين ساقط من الأصل، واستدركته من النسخ الأخرى.

(٥) ذكر وهب بن منبه أنه وجده في التوراة بلفظ: «يا من لا يستتم سرور يوم، ولا يأمن على روحه يومًا، الحذر الحذر».

رواه البيهقي في «الزهد الكبير» رقم (٥٢١)، وابن عساكر في «تاريخ دمشق» (٦٣/ ٣٩٣).

مرضت أبدانهم.

وقال بعض أهل العلم في الأثر المروي: «إذا رأيتم أهل البلاء فاسألوا الله العافية»[١]: إن أهل البلاء المبتلون بمعاصي الله والإعراض والغفلة عنه[٢].

وهذا وإن كان أعظم البلاء فاللفظ يتناول أنواع المبتلين في أبدانهم وأديانهم، والله أعلم.

الحادي عشر: أن يُعوِّد باعث الدين ودواعيه مصارعة الهوى ومقاومته على التدريج قليلاً قليلاً حتى يدرك لذة الظفر، فتقوى حينئذ هِمته، فإن من ذاق لذة شيء قويت همته في تحصيله. والاعتياد لممارسة الأعمال الشاقة يزيد القوى التي تصدر عنها تلك الأعمال، ولذلك تجد قوى الحمالين وأرباب الصنائع الشاقة تتزايد بخلاف البزاز[٣] والخياط ونحوهما. ومن ترك المجاهدة بالكلية ضعف فيه باعث الدين وقوي فيه باعث الشهوة، ومن عوّد نفسه مخالفة الهوى غلبه متى أراد.

---

(١) ذكر هذا الأثر ابن الجوزي في «المدهش» ص ٣٣٨، دون نسبة لأحد.
وجاء أنه مرفوع إلى النبي ﷺ كما سيأتي في الحاشية التالية، إلا أنه روي عن عيسى بن مريم أنه قال: «فارحموا أهل البلاء واحمدوا الله على العافية».
رواه: مالك في «الموطأ» (٢/ ٩٨٦) بلاغًا، ورواه ابن أبي شيبة في «مصنفه» رقم (٣١٨٧٩، ٣٤٢٣٠)، وأبو نعيم في «الحلية» (٦/ ٥٨، ٣٢٨) وغيرهما.

(٢) وهذا مروي عن الشبلي أنه سئل عن قول النبي ﷺ: «إذا رأيتم أهل البلاء فاسألوا الله العافية». من هم أهل البلاء؟ قال الشبلي: أهل الغفلة عن الله. انظر: «تاريخ بغداد» (١٢/ ١٦١).

(٣) البزاز هو بائع البَزّ. والبَزُّ: الثياب. «لسان العرب» (٥/ ٣١١ ـ ٣١٢).

١٠٦

الثاني عشر: كف الباطن عن حديث النفس، وإذا مرت به الخواطر نفاها ولا يؤويها ويساكنها، فإنها تصير مُنى، وهي رؤوسُ أموال المفاليس. ومتى ساكن الخواطر صارت أماني، ثم تقوى فتصير هموماً، ثم تقوى فتصير إرادات، ثم تقوى فتصير عزماً يقترن به المراد.

فدفع الخاطر الأول أسهل وأيسر من دفع أثر المقدور بعد وقوعه وترك معاودته(١).

الثالث عشر: قطع العلائق والأسباب التي تدعوه إلى موافقة الهوى، [٢٤/ ب] وليس المراد أن لا يكون له هوى، بل يصرف هواه إلى ما ينفعه ويستعمله في تنفيذ مراد الرب تعالى، فإن ذلك يدفع عنه شر استعماله في معاصيه، فإن كلَّ شيء من الإنسان يستعمله لله فإن الله يقيه شرّ استعماله لنفسه وللشيطان، وما لا يستعمله لله استعمله لنفسه وهواه ولا بد.

فالعلم إن لم يكن لله كان للنفس والهوى، والعمل إن لم يكن لله كان للرّياء والنفاق، والمال إن لم ينفق لله أنفق في طاعة الشيطان والهوى، والجاه إن لم يستعمل لله استعمل صاحبه في هواه وحظوظه، والقوة إن لم يستعملها في أمر الله استعملته في معصيته.

فمن عوّد نفسه العمل لله لم يكن عليه أشق من العمل لغيره، ومن عوّد نفسه العمل لهواه وحظه لم يكن عليه أشقّ من الإخلاص والعمل لله، وهذا في جميع أبواب الأعمال، فليس شيء أشق على المنفق لله

---

(١) توسع ابن القيم في بيان هذا الوجه في كتابه «طريق الهجرتين» ص ٢٧٤ وما بعدها.

من[1] الإنفاق لغيره، وكذا بالعكس.

الرابع عشر: صرف الفكر إلى عجائب آيات الله التي ندب عباده إلى التفكر فيها، وهي: آياته المتلوَّة وآياته المخلوقة، فإذا استولى ذلك على قلبه دفع عنه محاضرة الشيطان ومحادثته ووسواسه. وما أعظم غبن من أمكنه أن لا يزال محاضر الرحمن ورسوله والصحابة، فرغب عن ذلك إلى محاضرة الشيطان من الإنس والجنّ! فلا غبن بعد هذا الغبن، والله المستعان.

الخامس عشر: التفكر في الدنيا وسرعة زوالها وقرب انقضائها، فلا يرضى لنفسه أن يتزوّد منها إلى دار بقائه وخلوده أخسَّ ما فيها وأقله نفعًا [إلا ساقط الهمة دنيء المروءة ميت القلب][2] فإن حسرته تشتد إذا عاين حقيقة ما تزوده وتبين له عدم نفعه له، فكيف إذا كان زاده ما يعذب به ويناله بسببه غاية الألم؟! بل إذا تزود ما ينفعه وترك ما هو أنفع منه كان حسرة عليه.

السادس عشر: تعرضه إلى من القلوب بين إصبعيه، وأزمّة الأمور بيديه، وانتهاء كل شيء إليه على الدوام، فلعله أن يصادف أوقات النفحات، كما في الأثر المعروف: «إن لله في أيام دهره نفحات فتعرضوا لنفحاته، واسألوا الله أن يستُر عوراتكم، ويؤمن روعاتكم»[3].

---

(١) ليست في الأصل، وأثبتها من النسخ الثلاث الأخرى.

(٢) ما بين المعقوفين ساقط من الأصل، واستدركته من النسخ الثلاث الأخرى.

(٣) روي عن أبي الدرداء رضي الله عنه، رواه ابن أبي شيبة في «مصنفه» رقم (٣٤٥٩٤)، وأبو نعيم في «حلية الأولياء» (١/ ٢٢١).

وجاء في حديث مرفوع عن أنس بن مالك، أخرجه الطبراني في «الكبير» =

ولعله في كثرة تعرضه يصادف ساعة من الساعات التي لا يسأل الله فيها شيئًا إلا أعطاه، فمن أُعطي منشور الدعاء أُعطي الإجابة، [٢٥/ أ] فإنه لو لم يُرد إجابته لما ألهمه دعاءه، كما قيل:

لو لم ترِد نَيلَ ما أرجو وأطلبه ... من جود كفك ما عوّدتَني الطَّلبا[(١)]

ولا يستوحش مِنْ ظاهر الحال، فإن الله سبحانه يعامل عبده بمعاملة من ليس كمثله شيء في أفعاله، كما ليس كمثله شيء[(٢)] في صفاته، فإنه ما حَرَمه إلا ليعطيه، ولا أمرضه إلا ليشفيه، ولا أفقره إلا ليغنيه، ولا أماته إلا ليحييه، وما أخرج أبويه من الجنة إلا ليعيدهما إليها على أكمل حال، كما قيل: يا آدم لا تجزع من قولي لك: اخرُجْ منها، فلك خلقتها وسأعيدك إليها.

فالرب تعالى ينعم على عبده بابتلائه، ويعطيه بحرمانه، ويصحه بسقمه، فلا يستوحش عبده من حالة تسوؤه أصلًا إلا إذا كانت تغضبه عليه، وتبعده منه.

السابع عشر: أن يعلم بأن فيه جاذبين متضادين، ومحنته بين الجاذبين: جاذب يجذبه إلى الرفيق الأعلى من أهل عليين، وجاذب

= رقم (٧٢٠)، وأبو نعيم في «حلية الأولياء» (٣/ ١٦٢)، والبيهقي في «شعب الإيمان» رقم (١١٢١) وغيرهم.

وروي أيضًا من مسند أبي هريرة ومحمد بن مسلمة رضي الله عنهما. وحسنه الألباني مرفوعًا بمجموع طرقه وشواهده في «السلسلة الصحيحة» رقم (١٨٩٠).

(١) لم أقف عليه، وذكره ابن القيم رحمه الله في «مدارج السالكين» (٣/ ١٠٣).

(٢) كلمة «شيء» ساقطة من الأصل. واستدركتها من النسخ الثلاث الأخرى.

يجذبه إلى أسفل سافلين.

فكلما انقاد مع الجاذب الأعلى صعد درجة حتى ينتهي إلى حيث يليق به من المحل الأعلى، وكلما انقاد إلى الجاذب الأسفل نزل درجة حتى ينتهي إلى موضعه من سجين.

ومتى أراد أن يعلم هل هو مع الرفيق الأعلى أو الأسفل، فلينظر أين روحه في هذا العالم، فإنها إذا فارقت البدن تكون في الرفيق الذي كانت منجذبة إليه في الدنيا [فهو أولى بها، فالمرء مع من أحب طبعًا وعقلاً وجزاءً، وكل مهتم بشيء][1] فهو منجذب إليه وإلى أهله بالطبع، «وكلُّ امرىء يصبو إلى ما يناسبه»، وقد قال تعالى: ﴿ قُلْ كُلٌّ يَعْمَلُ عَلَىٰ شَاكِلَتِهِۦ ﴾ [الإسراء: ٨٤]، فالنفوس العلوية تنجذب بذاتها وهممها وأعمالها إلى أعلى، والنفوس السافلة إلى أسفل.

الثامن عشر: أن يعلم أن تفريغ المحل شرط لنزول غيث[2] الرحمة، وتنقيته من الدغل[3] شرط لكمال الزرع، فمتى لم يفرغ المحل لم يصادف غيث الرحمة محلاً فارغًا قابلاً[4] ينزل فيه، وإن فرّغه حتى أصابه غيث الرحمة لكنه لم يُنَقِّه من الدّغل لم يكن الزرع زرعًا كاملاً بل ربما غلب الدّغل على الزرع وكان الحكم له.

---

(١) ما بين المعقوفين ساقط من الأصل، واستدركته من النسخ الثلاث الأخرى.

(٢) ليست في الأصل، وإنما أثبتها من النسخ الأخرى، وهو مفهوم مما يأتي في كلام المصنف.

(٣) الدَّغَل: الفساد، وأصل الدّغل الشجر الملتف الكثير. انظر: «لسان العرب» (١١/ ٢٤٤ ـ ٢٤٥).

(٤) الكلمتان: «فارغًا قابلاً» ليستا في الأصل. أما الكلمة الأولى فهي من: (م) و (ن). وأما الكلمة الثانية، فهي من باقي النسخ.

١١٠

وهذا كالذي يصلح أرضه، ويهيئها لقبول الزرع، ويودع فيها البذر، وينتظر نزول الغيث، فإذا طهّر العبد قلبه وفرّغه من إرادات السوء وخواطره، وبذر فيه بذر الذكر والفكر والمحبة [٢٥/ ب] والإخلاص، وعرّضه لمهاب رياح الرحمة، وانتظر نزول غيث الرحمة في أوانه، كان جديرًا في حصول المُغَلّ(١).

وكما يقوى الرجاء لنزول الغيث في وقته، كذلك يقوى الرجاء لإصابة نفحات الرحمن جل جلاله في الأوقات الفاضلة والأحوال الشريفة، ولا سيما إذا اجتمعت الهمم، وتساعدت القلوب، وعظم الجمع، كجمع عرفة وجمع الاستسقاء وجمع أهل الجمعة، فإن اجتماع الهمم والأنفاس أسباب نصبها الله تعالى مقتضية لحصول الخير ونزول الرحمة، كما نصب سائر الأسباب مُفضِية إلى مسبَّباتها.

بل هذه الأسباب في حصول الرحمة، أقوى من الأسباب الحسية في حصول مسبّباتها، ولكن العبد لجهله يغلب عليه الشاهد على الغائب والحس على العقل، ولظلمه يؤثر ما يحكم به هذا ويقتضيه على ما يحكم به الآخر ويقتضيه، ولو فرّغ العبد المحل وهيأه وأصلحه لرأى العجائب، فإن فضل الله لا يرده إلا المانع الذي في العبد، فلو أزال ذلك المانع لسارع إليه الفضل من كل صوب. فتأمل حال نهر عظيم يسقي كل أرض يمر عليها، فحصل بينه وبين بعض الأرض المعطشة المُجدبة سكْرٌ(٢) وسدّ كثيف، فصاحبها يشكو الجدب، والنهر إلى جانب أرضه!

---

(١) الأصل: «الممغل»، وما أثبت من النسخ الأخرى هو الصواب. والمغلّ بمعنى الغَلَّة.

(٢) قال في «لسان العرب» (٤/ ٣٧٥): سَكَرَ النهرَ يَسْكُرُه سَكْرًا: سَدّ فاه، وكل =

١١١

التاسع عشر: أن يعلم العبد أن الله سبحانه خلقه لبقاء لا فناء له، ولعز لا ذُلَّ معه، وأمن لا خوف فيه، وغناء لا فقر معه، ولذّة لا ألم معها، وكمال لا نقص فيه، وامتحنه في هذه الدار بالبقاء الذي يسرع إليه الفناء، والعز الذي يقارنه الذلُّ ويعقبه الذلُّ، والأمن الذي معه الخوف وبعده الخوف، وكذلك الغناء واللذة والفرحة والسرور والنعيم الذي هنا مشوب بضدّه يتعقبه ضدّه، وهو سريع الزوال، فغَلِطَ أكثر الخلق في هذا المقام إذ طلبوا النعيم والبقاء والعز والملك والجاه في غير محله، ففاتهم في محله، وأكثرهم لم يظفر بما طلبه من ذلك، والذي ظفر به إنما هو متاع قليل ثم يزول عنه.

والرسل إنما جاءوا بالدعوة إلى النعيم المقيم والملك الكبير، فمن أجابهم حصل له ألذ ما في الدنيا وأطيبه [٢٦/ أ] فكان عيشه فيها أطيب من عيش الملوك فمن دونهم، فإن الزهد في الدنيا ملك حاضر، والشيطان يحسد المؤمن عليه أعظم حسد، فيحرص كل الحرص على أن لا يصل إليه، فإن العبد إذا ملك شهوته وغضبه فانقادا معه لداعي الدين فهو الملك حقًّا؛ لأن صاحب هذا الملك حرٌّ، والمَلِك المنقاد لشهوته وغضبه عبد شهوته وغضبه، فهو مسخَّر مملوك في زي مالك، يقوده زمام الشهوة والغضب، كما يقاد البعير.

فالمغرور المخدوع يقعُ نظره على المُلْكِ[١] الظاهر الذي صورته مُلكٌ وباطنه رقّ، وعلى الشهوة التي أولها لذة وآخرها حسرة.

= شَق سُدّ فقد سُكِر، والسِّكْرُ: ما سُدّ به.

(١) ليست في الأصل، وأثبتها من النسخ الأخرى.

١١٢

والبصير الموفق يغير نظره من الأوائل إلى الأواخر، ومن المبادىء إلى العواقب، وذلك فضل الله يؤتيه من يشاء، والله ذو الفضل العظيم.

العشرون: أن لا يغترّ باعتقاده أن مجرد العلم بما ذكرنا كافٍ في حصول المقصود، بل لا بد أن يضيف إليه بذل الجهد في استعماله واستفراغ الوسع والطاقة فيه. وملاك ذلك الخروج عن العوائد فإنها أعداء الكمال والفلاح، فلا أفلح من استمرّ على عوائده أبدًا. ويستعين على الخروج عن العوائد بالهرب عن مظان الفتنة والبعد منها، قال النبي ﷺ: **«من سمع بالدجال فلينأ عنه»**[1]، فما استعين على التخلص من الشر بمثل البعد عن أسبابه ومظانّه.

وهاهنا لطيفة للشيطان لا يتخلص منها إلا حاذق، وهي: أن يظهر له في مظان الشر بعض[2] شيء من الخير، ويدعوه إلى تحصيله، فإذا قرب منه ألقاه في الشبكة، والله المستعان[3].

---

(١) أخرجه أبو داود في «سننه» رقم (٤٣١٩) من حديث عمران بن حصين رضي الله عنه. وصححه الحاكم في «المستدرك» (٤/ ٥٣١) على شرط مسلم.

(٢) في الأصل: «ضد»، والتصويب من (ب).

(٣) هذا الباب الذي هو في الأسباب التي تعين على الصبر، بشقّيه: تضعيف باعث الشهوة، وتقوية باعث الدين، قد اقتبسه الإمام ابن القيم رحمه الله من الإمام الغزالي في كتابه «إحياء علوم الدين» (٤/ ٦٥) وما بعدها. وبالطبع قد زاد الإمام ابن القيم هنا أمورًا تضرب لها أكباد الإبل.

١١٣

The Actual Words of Imām Ibn al-Qayyim

Strengthening of the religious motivational factors can occur in the following ways:

1. To revere *Allāh* (تَبَارَكَ وَتَعَالَى) so that He is not disobeyed, while He sees and He hears. Whoever actualizes this reverence of *Allāh* with his heart, then his heart will not consent to him [disobeying *Allāh*].

2. Consciousness of the love of *Allāh* (سُبْحَانَهُ وَتَعَالَى). So he will abandon His disobedience out of his love for Him. For indeed the lover obeys his beloved. And the best type of renunciation is that of lovers, just as the best obedience is the obedience of lovers. There is a big difference between the renunciation and obedience of a lover and the renunciation and obedience of the one afraid of punishment.

3. Consciousness of the blessing and favor, as verily the noble person does not repay the one who treated him well with discourtesy. This is a trait of ignoble people. Therefore, the acknowledgement of the blessing and favor of *Allāh*, should prevent him from disobeying Him because he is shy that *Allāh's* favors and blessings descend upon him, while his disobedience, sins and evil acts are rising to His Lord. So an angel descends with one thing [i.e. blessings] and another angel ascends with another [i.e. evil deeds]. What a wretched exchange!

4. Consciousness of the anger and wrath of *Allāh*. Indeed the Lord, the Most High, is angry when the servant persists to disobey Him. If He is angry, then nothing can withstand His anger, let alone this weak servant.

5. Consciousness of the loss [this involves]. This is the loss of the good of this world and the Hereafter, which result from disobedience. And the dishonorable titles, according to the religion, intellect and custom that are given to him; and the praiseworthy titles he loses as a consequence of this.

As it pertains to this point of reflection, then it is sufficient to recognize the decrease of faith - an atom of which is far better than this world and what it contains. How can he sell it in exchange for desires? The elation of which will soon vanish but the evil consequences will remain, and the lust will vanish and misery will remain.

It is authentically reported from the Prophet (صَلَّىٰ ٱللَّهُ عَلَيْهِ وَسَلَّمَ) that he said, "The adulterer who commits adultery is not a believer while he is committing adultery."

Some of the Companions said, "Faith is removed from him and remains hovering over his head like a canopy. If he repents, then it returns to him."

Some of the Tābiʿūn stated, "Belief is removed from him as a shirt is taken off. If he repents, he wears it again,"

The Prophet (صَلَّىٰ ٱللَّهُ عَلَيْهِ وَسَلَّمَ) saw, as is found in the hadith reported by Bukharī, the adulterers in the oven, naked. This is because they took off the garment of faith, and the oven of lust which was burning in their hearts will become a real oven that burns with the fire.

6. The consciousness of suppression and victory. If the servant suppresses his desires and conquers the devil, then he will experience sweetness, happiness, and delight greater and sweeter than that obtained from the defeat of one's human enemies. The

end result of this is like taking beneficial medicine that removes the illness of the body and returns it to health and homeostasis.

7. Consciousness of the compensation and reward. This is the compensation that *Allāh* (سُبْحَانَهُ وَتَعَالَىٰ) has promised for people who abandon forbidden matters for His sake and prevent their souls from their desires. [The servant] should compare the compensation to that which it replaces, and whatever of the two is more rewarding, then he should choose it and be pleased with it for himself.

8. Consciousness of the *maʿiyyah* of *Allāh* and it is of two types: general *maʿiyyah* and specific *maʿiyyah*.

   The general *maʿiyyah* of *Allāh* is that His Lord sees him [and is aware of everything], and that he is before His Eye and none of his affairs are hidden from Him. This has been explained earlier.

   The intent here is the specific *maʿiyyah* of *Allāh*, as found in His Saying,

   "Indeed, *Allāh* is with the patient." (Al-Anfāl: 46)

   "Indeed, *Allāh* is with those who fear Him and those who are doers of good." (Al-Naḥl: 128)

   "And indeed, *Allāh* is with the doers of good." (Al-ʿAnkabūt: 69)

   The specific *maʿiyyah* of *Allāh* is better and more beneficial to the individual in this world and the hereafter than him satisfying his lusts and fulfilling his desires completely from the beginning of his life to its end.

So how can a person give preference to a brief period of pleasure in one's life that is spoiled and arduous, which is only like the dreams of the sleeping and a moving shadow?

9. Consciousness of an unexpected death and early end. This is for a person to fear that death will suddenly come upon him and thus *Allāh* will take [his soul] unexpectedly. So he is deprived of what he covets of the delights of this life and he is deprived of what he covets of the delights of the hereafter. What a great misfortune! How bitter and hard this is? However, no one is aware of this except the one who experienced it. It is found in some of the previous books:

   "O you who is not secure for the blink of an eye and who is incompetent of attaining the happiness of a day, be very cautious."

10. Consciousness of the calamity and wellbeing. Indeed calamity in reality is nothing except sin and its consequences, while complete wellbeing is obedience and its consequences. The people who are afflicted with these calamities are the people of disobedience, even if their bodies are healthy. And the people who are in a state of wellbeing are the people of obedience, even though their bodies are sick.

    Some of the people of knowledge said concerning the narration that has been reported: "When you see a people who have been afflicted, then ask *Allāh* for wellbeing." This is because those who are afflicted with calamities are those who have been tested with the disobedience of *Allāh*, turning away from Him and heedlessness of Him.

    Although this is the greatest type of affliction, then the wording encompasses the various types of people who are afflicted in their bodies and their religions. *Allāh* knows best.

11. That he gets accustomed to the implementation of the religious motivational factors and methods to struggle and battle against lusts gradually, bit by bit, until he grasps the ecstasy of victory and thus his resolve strengthens. Verily when a person tastes the ecstasy of something his resolve to achieve it strengthens. Just like getting accustomed to burdensome work increases one's strength that is required for these jobs. You find the baggage carriers and those engaged in manual labor increases, unlike cloth traders, tailors and the like.

    So totally abandoning the struggle [against the soul] weakens the influence of the religious motivational factors and the drive of desire strengthens within a person. Whoever accustoms himself to countering his desires, then he will be able to overwhelm them whenever he chooses.

12. Repelling evil thoughts from the soul. If these sort of thoughts come to his mind, he should block them and not allow them to settle and develop. Once they settle, they turn into aspirations, which are the assets of the ruined. When these thoughts settle they become aspirations that develop and become intentions; then they grow further and develop into a will. Finally, they become a determination, which is associated with the envisioned act itself. Therefore, it is easier and simpler to repel these initial thoughts and to not get accustomed to them, instead of trying to prevent the effects of what has been decreed after it has occurred.

13. Severance of all relationships and reasons that incite him to follow his desires. The objective is to not eradicate these desires altogether, rather for him to redirect his desires towards that which is beneficial for him and to utilize them to carry out the orders of the Lord, the Most High. Indeed this will repel from him the evil of employing his desires to disobey *Allāh*.

Whenever a person utilizes something for the sake of *Allāh*, then verily *Allāh* safeguards him from this being abused by his soul and the devil. So if knowledge is not used for the sake of *Allāh*, then it will be used for the soul and his desires. The same applies to actions; if they are not solely for *Allāh*, then they will be performed to show off and out of hypocrisy. If money is not spent for the sake of *Allāh*, then it will be spent in obedience to the devil and desires.

If a position is not used by the individual for the sake of *Allāh*, then it will be exploited to fulfil his desires and whims. If power and strength is not used to implement the command of *Allāh*, then it will be used for His disobedience. Whoever accustoms himself to act solely for the sake of *Allāh*, then he will find nothing more difficult than doing something for other than His sake; and if someone accustoms himself to act in accordance to his desires and wishes, then he will find nothing more difficult than sincerity and acting solely for the sake of *Allāh*. This is true for all forms of actions. There is nothing harder for someone who spends in *Allāh*'s cause than spending for other than *Allāh*, and vice versa.

14. Contemplating over the amazing signs of *Allāh*, which He commands His servants to reflect upon, and they are His recited verses and His created signs. If this reflection occupies his heart, then this repels the speech, whisperings and talk of the devil. What greater loss is there for the one who is able to benefit from the words of *Allāh*, His Messenger and the companions but turns away from this to listen to the speech of the devils from the Jinn and humans?! There is no loss greater than this – and *Allāh's* aid is sought.

15. To think about the reality of this world, the swiftness of its passing and the nearness of its end. No one is content to take as a provision for his permanent and eternal abode the most despicable and least

beneficial things from this world, except the person who possesses low resolve, lacks dignity and has a dead heart. Indeed his regret will increase when he sees the real worth of the provisions he prepared and when he recognizes their worthlessness. So how much [more sorrow will he feel] if he takes something that is a cause for his punishment and for which he will suffer excruciating pain? He will even feel regret if he acquires useful provisions yet abandons something more beneficial.

16. To turn to the One who has the hearts of the servants between His two fingers, Who the control of everything is in His two hands and Who everything returns to on a consistent basis. It is possible that he may find the moment when bounties are bestowed, as is found in the narration,

"*Allāh* has particular days throughout time for bestowing His gift, so seek these times and ask *Allāh* to conceal your faults and safeguard you from fears."

It is possible that through his regular turning to *Allāh*, he may find an hour from the hours in which if he asked *Allāh* for something then *Allāh* would grant it. Whoever is granted the opportunity to supplicate to *Allāh* correctly, then his supplication will be answered, as if He did not want to answer the supplication of the servant He would not have inspired him to supplicate, as it is said in the proverbial saying,

"If you did not want me to acquire what I had hoped for and sought from your generosity, then you would have not accustomed me to asking."

The servant should not lose hope due to the [difficulties] of the apparent situation. For indeed *Allāh* treats His servant in the manner of One who has none like him as it pertains to His actions, just as there is none like Him in His Attributes. He did not deprive the servant except to give him, He did not make him sick except to cure him, He did not place him in poverty except to make him rich, and He did not give death except to resurrect him. He did not remove his parents from paradise except to re-enter them into paradise in the most perfect fashion, as it was said: "O Adam, do not be worried by my Saying, 'Leave from here.' I have created you for paradise and I will return you to it."

The Lord, the Most High, blesses His servant by testing him: He gives him after deprivation and cures him after sickness. His servant should never lose hope due to a state he dislikes, unless it causes *Allāh* to be angry with him and distances him from *Allāh.*

17. The servant should know that he has two opposing forces and that he is being pulled by each force in the opposite directions. One force is pulling him towards the Loftiest Companion, whereas the other force is pulling him to the lowest of the low.

Whenever he is steered by the higher force, he ascends a degree until he reaches a suitable place, which is a lofty station. Conversely, whenever he yields to the lower force, he descends a degree until he reaches his place in *Sijjīn.*

If he desires to know whether his place will be with the Loftiest Companion or the lowest, then let him look where his spirit is in the life of this world. As when the spirits departs from the body it will be with the companion that it was attracted to in this world, as they are more deserving of it.

A person is with the one whom he loves, according to nature, logic and recompense; and everyone who is fascinated by something is naturally drawn to it and its people. "Everyone will be drawn to whatever suits them."

Allāh said,

"Say, 'Each works according to his manner.'" (Al-Isrā': 84)

The higher souls are attracted with their essence, resolve and actions to what is noble and lofty, and the lower souls towards what is lowly and ignoble.

18. To know that it is a condition for the land to be cleared for the descent of the rain of mercy and for it to be purified of weeds is a prerequisite to allow the plants to grow perfectly. If the land is not empty, then the rain of mercy will not find a clear, suitable place to descend upon.

And if the place is cleared in order for the rain of mercy to descend upon it; however, it is not cleansed of weeds, then the vegetation will not grow properly. It is possible for the weeds to engulf the vegetation and establish its rule [upon the water supply and nutrients].

The similitude of this is like a man who prepares his land and primes it for planting vegetation. So he plants the seeds and waits for the rain to fall. Similarly, if the servant purifies his heart and removes from it evil intentions and thoughts, and he sows in it the seeds of remembrance, reflection, love and sincerity; and exposes it to the treasured winds of mercy and waits for the rain of mercy to descend in its time, then he is deserving to reap the harvest.

Just as the hope for rainfall increases at its expected time, then so does the hope for receiving the favors of the Most Merciful (جَلَّ جَلَالُهُ) grow stronger during the virtuous times and noble settings. Especially, if this is coupled with resolve and determination, the hearts are supporting one another and it is a large gathering like the congregation at *'Arafah*, the congregation for the prayer for rain, or the congregation for the Friday prayer. The gathering of determinations and souls are causes that *Allāh*, the Most High, has set for the attainment of good and the descent of mercy, just as He has set causes that produce their established effects.

Actually, the above causes for the attainment of mercy are stronger than the perceptible causes that produce their fixed results. However, the servant due to his ignorance, is swayed more by what is visible than what is hidden, and by what is perceptible more than reason.

And due to his oppression he prefers that which is determined and required by that which is physical over what is determined and required by that which is hidden. If the servant was to clean the area, prepare it and rectify it, then he would witness remarkable things.

Verily, nothing can prevent the grace of *Allāh* except the barriers found within the servant himself. If he removed these obstacles, then this grace would hasten to him from every direction. Consider the example of a vast river that waters every land through which it passes; however, there was a barrier and a large dam between it and parts of the land. So the owner of this land complains of drought while the river flows beside his land.

19. To know that *Allāh* (سُبْحَانَهُ وَتَعَالَى) has created the servant for eternal existence without conclusion, honor void of disgrace, security void of fear, affluence void of poverty, delight void of pain and perfection free from defect. He tests him in this world with life that quickly comes to an end, with honor accompanied by disgrace and followed by disgrace, and with security mixed with fear and followed by trepidation. The same can be said about

affluence, enjoyment, happiness, joy and comfort, all of them are tarnished [in this life] with their opposites and succeeded by their opposites. They disappear quickly. The majority of the creation err in this matter, as they seek bliss, eternity, honor, power, dominion and position in the wrong place. So they miss out on these things in their rightful place. The majority of them do not successfully attain what they are searching for and those do only achieve a brief enjoyment, which vanishes quickly.

The Messengers of Allāh (عَلَيْهِمُ السَّلَامُ) came with the call to eternal comfort and to the great kingdom. Whoever responds to them will receive the greatest enjoyment of this world and the most pleasant of what exists therein. His life in this world is more pleasant than the life of the kings and anyone else. Indeed abstention in this life is an existing dominion.

This is something that the devil envies the believer for with the greatest envy, and he strives in every way possible to deprive the believer of this. If the servant controls his desires and anger, and if they yield to the call of the religion, then he is a true king. This is because the possessor of this dominion is free and independent, whereas the king who surrenders to his desires and anger is a captive of his lusts and anger. So in reality he is a subservient subject in the attire of a king who is being steered by the reins of lust and anger, as a camel is led.

The person who is deceived and deluded focusses his sight solely upon the visible dominion, which appears like a kingdom but in reality is nothing more than slavery, and upon the lusts that initially are pleasurable but in the end are regretful. On the other hand, the astute and successful individual changes the focus of his vision from the beginnings to the end, and from the causes to the consequences, and this is from the grace of *Allāh*, which He grants to whomsoever He wishes. Allāh is the owner of great bounty.

20. He should not be deluded by his belief that mere knowledge of what we have mentioned is sufficient to reach the desired goal. Rather, it is incumbent that he exerts effort to apply this knowledge and that he gives his utmost exertion and ability to do so. The pivotal factor is the abandonment of accustomed practices, because they are enemies of perfection and success. There is no success for a person who cannot rid himself of his habits, ever. He should seek assistance to rid himself of these habits by fleeing from the sources of Fitnah and staying far away from them.

The Messenger of *Allāh* (صَلَّىٰ ٱللَّٰهُ عَلَيْهِ وَسَلَّمَ) said:

"Whoever hears about the *Dajjāl* should flee from him."

Nothing aids [the servant] to escape evil like avoiding its sources and causes.

It is appropriate to mention a trick of the devil, which no one escapes except for the wise. This is that he attempts to present some good in the sources of evil and thus he calls people to partake in it. So when they approach it he catches them in this net – and the aid of *Allāh* is sought.

Appendix 1
The Prayer of Repentance
Salāh al-Tawbah
Its Description and Rulings

"The Muslim should endeavor to fear Allāh (سُبْحَانَهُ وَتَعَالَى), be conscious that Allāh is aware of his behavior and abstain from committing acts of disobedience. If he was to sin, then he should hasten to repent and turn to Allāh in penitence.

The Prophet (صَلَّى ٱللَّٰهُ عَلَيْهِ وَعَلَىٰ آلِهِ وَسَلَّمَ) legislated this prayer at the time of repentance."[1]

Abū Bakr (رَضِيَ ٱللَّٰهُ عَنْهُ) said I heard the Messenger of Allāh (صَلَّى ٱللَّٰهُ عَلَيْهِ وَعَلَىٰ آلِهِ وَسَلَّمَ) say,

مَا مِنْ رَجُلٍ يُذْنِبُ ذَنْبًا، ثُمَّ يَقُومُ فَيَتَطَهَّرُ، ثُمَّ يُصَلِّي، ثُمَّ يَسْتَغْفِرُ اللَّهَ، إِلَّا غَفَرَ اللَّهُ لَهُ» ثُمَّ قَرَأَ هَذِهِ الآيَةَ: {وَالَّذِينَ إِذَا فَعَلُوا فَاحِشَةً أَوْ ظَلَمُوا أَنْفُسَهُمْ ذَكَرُوا اللَّهَ فَاسْتَغْفَرُوا لِذُنُوبِهِمْ}

"There is not a man who commits a sin then purifies himself, stands and prays [two *rak'ah*][2], and then asks Allāh for forgiveness except that Allāh will forgive him. Then he recited this verse:

---

[1] Taken from *Bugyah al-Mutaṭawi'* (p. 119-120) of Shaykh Muḥammad Bazmūl.

[2] The wording "two *rak'ah*" is found in the version of this ḥadīth collected by Abū Dāwūd (no. 1521), Ibn Mājah (no. 390) and others.

﴿ وَٱلَّذِينَ إِذَا فَعَلُوا۟ فَٰحِشَةً أَوْ ظَلَمُوٓا۟ أَنفُسَهُمْ ذَكَرُوا۟ ٱللَّهَ فَٱسْتَغْفَرُوا۟
لِذُنُوبِهِمْ ﴿١٣٥﴾ ﴾

'And those who, when they have committed *Fāḥishah* (illegal sexual intercourse) or wronged themselves with evil, remember Allāh and ask forgiveness for their sins... [Āl-'Imrān 3:135]."[1]

Salāh al-Tawbah

A number of the scholars, past and present, have referred to this prayer as the prayer of repentance (*Salāh al-Tawbah*). From them is Ibn Qudāmah in *al-Mughnī* (2/553), Ibn Taymīyah in *Majmū' al-Fatāwa* (23/215), al-Mundhirī in *al-Targhīb Wa al-Tarhīb*, al-Suyūṭī in *al-Iklīl* (p. 56), Ibn Bāz in his *al-Fatāwa* (11/420) and numerous others.

فصل : في صَلاةِ التَّوبةِ : عن عليٍّ ، رَضِيَ اللهُ عنه ، قال : حَدَّثني أبو بكرٍ ،
وصَدَقَ أبو بكرٍ ، قال : سمعتُ رسولَ اللهِ ﷺ يقول : « ما مِن رَجُلٍ يُذْنِبُ ذَنْبًا ،
ثُمَّ يَقُومُ فَيَتَطَهَّرُ ، ثُمَّ يُصَلِّي رَكْعَتَيْنِ ، ثُمَّ يَسْتَغْفِرُ اللهَ تَعالَى إلَّا غَفَرَ له » . ثم قرأ

Ibn Qudāmah in al Mughnī (2/553)

Imām Ibn Qudāmah (رَحِمَهُ ٱللَّهُ) said,

"Chapter: Concerning the Prayer of Repentance." Under this chapter he mentions the ḥadīth narrated by Abu Bakr.

[1] **Ḥasan:** Collected by al-Tirmidhī (no. 406) with this wording, Abū Dāwūd (no. 1521), Ibn Mājah (no. 390) and others. This ḥadīth was declared ḥasan by Shaykh al-Albānī in Ṣaḥīḥ Sunan al-Tirmidhī (1/128). Shaykh Aḥmad Shākir held this hadith to be Ṣaḥīḥ in 'Umdah al-Tafsīr (1/417).

Shaykh al-Islām Ibn Taymīyah (رَحِمَهُ ٱللَّهُ) stated,

وحديث صلاة التوبة محفوظ فى السنن عن على، عن أبى بكر
الصديق، عن النبى صلى الله عليه وسلم أنه قال: «ما من مسلم
يذنب ذنبا فيتوضأ (٣) ويحسن الوضوء، ثم يصلّى ركعتين ويستغفر الله
إلا غفر له» وقرأ هذه الآية: [﴿والَّذِينَ إِذَا فَعَلُوا فَاحِشَةً أَوْ ظَلَمُوا
أَنفُسَهُمْ ذَكَرُوا اللَّهَ﴾ [سورة آل عمران: ١٣٥]](٤).

Al- Istiqāmah (2/18

"The ḥadīth pertaining to *Salāh al-Tawbah* is preserved in the *Sunan* by way of ʿAlī Abū Ṭālib from Abū Bakr who narrated it from the Prophet (صَلَّى ٱللَّهُ عَلَيْهِ وَعَلَىٰ آلِهِ وَسَلَّمَ)..."[1]

Al-ʿAllāmah Ibn Bāz (رَحِمَهُ ٱللَّهُ) said,

"As for *Salāh al-Tawbah*, then it is established upon the Prophet (صَلَّى ٱللَّهُ عَلَيْهِ وَعَلَىٰ آلِهِ وَسَلَّمَ) by way of the (ḥadīth) of al-Ṣiddīq (رَضِيَ ٱللَّهُ عَنْهُ)..."[2]

Al-Ḥāfiẓ Ibn Ḥajr (رَحِمَهُ ٱللَّهُ) in *al-Fatḥ* (11/98) said,

وقد ورد فى حديث حسن صفة الاستغفار المشار اليه فى الآية أخرجه أحمد والاربعة وصححه ابن حبان من حديث
على بن أبى طالب قال : حدثنى أبو بكر الصديق رضى الله عنهما وصدق أبو بكر : سمعت النبى ﷺ يقول : ما من
رجل يذنب ذنبا ثم يقوم فيتطهر فيحسن الطهور ثم يستغفر الله عز وجل إلا غفر له ، ثم تلا ﴿ والذين إذا

Al-Fatḥ (11/98)

"There comes in a ḥadīth, which is ḥasan, a description of the modus of seeking forgiveness that was alluded to in this verse. It has been collected by Aḥmad and by the four [Imāms of ḥadīth];

[1] *Al-Istiqāmah* (2/184).

[2] *Majmūʿ Fatāwa* Ibn Bāz (11/420).

it was declared Ṣaḥīḥ by Ibn Ḥibbān. It was narrated by ʿAlī Abū Ṭālib (رَضِيَ ٱللَّٰهُ عَنْهُ) that he said,

ʿAbū Bakr (رَضِيَ ٱللَّٰهُ عَنْهُ) narrated to me, and Abu Bakr (رَضِيَ ٱللَّٰهُ عَنْهُ) spoke the truth, that he heard the Prophet (صَلَّى ٱللَّٰهُ عَلَيْهِ وَعَلَىٰ آلِهِ وَسَلَّمَ) say,

ما من رجل يذنب ذنبا ثم يقوم فيتطهر فيحسن الطهور ثم يستغفر الله عز وجل
إِلَّا غفر له ثم تلا وَالَّذِينَ إذا فعلوا فاحشة الآية

"There is not a man who commits a sin then purifies himself correctly, stands and prays, and then asks Allāh for forgiveness except that he is forgiven. Then he recited this verse: "And those who, when they have committed *Fāḥishah* (illegal sexual intercourse)…""""

Al-Suyūṭī (رَحِمَهُ ٱللَّٰهُ) stated,

قوله تعالى: والذين إذا فعلوا فاحشة أو ظلموا أنفسهم ، فيه مشروعية صلاة التوبة
وأخرج أحمد وأصحاب السنن وابن حبان وغيرهم عن علي قال حدثني أبو بكر أن
رسول الله صلى الله عليه وسلم قال « ما من عبد يذنب ذنباً ثم يتوضأ ويصلي ركعتين
ويستغفر الله إلا غفر له » ثم تلا هذه الآية: والذين إذا فعلوا فاحشة أو ظلموا أنفسهم
ذكروا الله فاستغفروا لذنوبهم .

Al-Iklīl (p. 56)

"His Saying,

﴿ وَٱلَّذِينَ إِذَا فَعَلُوا۟ فَٰحِشَةً أَوْ ظَلَمُوٓا۟ أَنفُسَهُمْ ﴾

In this is a proof that *Salāh al-Tawbah* is legislated. Aḥmad, the collectors of the *Sunan*, Ibn Ḥibbān and others reported upon the authority of Ali that he said…"

The ruling of this prayer

"It is highly recommended (*mandūb*) for him to pray two *rak'ah* and then repent, as comes in the ḥadīth of Abū Bakr (رَضِيَ ٱللَّهُ عَنْهُ)..."

Al-Ḥāfiẓ Ibn Kathīr (رَحِمَهُ ٱللَّهُ) stated in his Tafsīr,

> "It is highly recommended to perform *Wuḍū* and pray two *rak'ah* when repenting based upon the ḥadīth collected by Imām Aḥmad upon 'Alī...This ḥadīth is *ḥasan*."[1]

Description of this prayer

It comprises of two *rak'ah* as established in the aforementioned ḥadīth of Abū Bakr (رَضِيَ ٱللَّهُ عَنْهُ).

There is no proof to support the recitation of specific *Sūrahs* or *Āyāt* in this prayer, and Allāh knows best.

It is to be prayed before repentance

The strongest position is that the prayer of repentance is to be prayed prior to repentance, as mentioned by Ibn Taymīyah (رَحِمَهُ ٱللَّهُ) when he said,

> "It is recommended (*mandūb*) for him to pray two *rak'ah* and **then** repent, as comes in the ḥadīth of Abū Bakr (رَضِيَ ٱللَّهُ عَنْهُ)..."

This is supported by the apparent wording of the ḥadīth narrated by Abū Bakr because prayer was mentioned prior to asking for

[1] *Tafsīr Ibn Kathīr* (2/108).

forgiveness; the word ثم indicates that seeking forgiveness is after the prayer.

Is it permissible to pray the prayer of repentance during the prohibited times?

The prayer of repentance is considered to be from those prayers that are prayed for a specific reason (*Dhawāt al-Asbāb*).[1] If the servant was to sin at this time, then it is obligatory upon him to repent immediately. So if he was to pray during a prohibited period of time, then this is permissible.[2]

The reason for the prayer of repentance?

Shaykh al-Islam Ibn Taymīyah (رَحِمَهُ ٱللَّهُ) stated when talking about the prayers that are prayed for a reason,

> "Likewise the prayer of repentance. If he was to sin, then it is obligatory for him to repent immediately. It is highly recommended (*mandūb*) for him to pray two rak'ah and then repent, as comes in the ḥadīth of Abū Bakr (رَضِيَ ٱللَّهُ عَنْهُ)..."[3]

Is the prayer of repentance a means to draw nearer to Allāh through righteous actions?

This is *tawassul* (seeking a means to draw nearer to Allāh) through one's actions, because *tawassul* can be through speech and action. So the fact

[1] Majmū' al-Fatāwa (23/215).
[2] Refer to the explanation of *Sunan al-Tirmidhī* of Shaykh 'Abd al-Muḥsin al-'Abād. The Book of Prayer. Chapter: What Has Been Related Concerning Praying When Repenting. (00.20.47)
[3] Majmū' al-Fatāwa (23/215).

that the individual is praying to Allāh (عَزَّوَجَلَّ) prior to supplicating to Allāh and asking Him for forgiveness is no doubt from the reasons for this to be accepted.[1]

It is not a condition of repentance to pray Salāh al-Tawbah

"It is not a prerequisite for the correctness of one's repentance that you pray two rakʿah. Rather, it is a condition to refrain from the sin, be resolute never to return to it, have remorse for what transpired and absolve oneself from the rights of the creation.

However, whoever purifies them self, prays two rakʿah and then repents to Allāh, having remorse for what has occurred, refraining from this (sin) and truly resolute to never return to it, then this is more complete and closer to this repentance being accepted.

This is based upon the ḥadīth authentically established by way of Abū Bakr (رَضِيَٱللَّهُعَنْهُ) who said that the Prophet (صَلَّىٱللَّهُعَلَيْهِوَعَلَىٰآلِهِوَسَلَّمَ) said,

مَا مِنْ رَجُلٍ يُذْنِبُ ذَنْبًا فَيَتَوَضَّأُ فَيُحْسِنُ الْوُضُوءَ، ثُمَّ يُصَلِّي رَكْعَتَيْنِ، فَيَسْتَغْفِرُ اللهَ عَزَّ وَجَلَّ إِلَّا غُفِرَ لَهُ

"There is not a man who commits a sin then performs *Wuḍū* correctly, stands and prays two rakʿah and then asks Allāh (عَزَّوَجَلَّ) for forgiveness except that he will be forgiven." Collected by Aḥmad in al-Musnad."[2]

[1] Explanation of *Sunan al-Tirmidhī* by Shaykh ʿAbd al-Muḥsin al-ʿAbād. The Book of Prayer. Chapter: What Has Been Related Concerning Praying When Repenting. (00.16.17)

[2] *Fatāwa al-Lajnah al-Dā'imah* (24/310). Shaykh Ibn Bāz (رَحِمَهُٱللَّهُ) was the head of the committee at the time.

Al-ʿAllāmah Ṣāliḥ al-Fawzān (حفظه الله) was asked,

> "My companion said to me that if you want to repent then you should go and perform *Wuḍū* and then pray two *rakʿah*; and that this prayer is called *Ṣalāh al-Tawbah*. Is this action correct?"

He (حفظه الله) responded:

> "Yes, there is a hadith found pertaining to this. If a person does this: performs *Wuḍū*, prays two *rakʿah* and then repents to Allāh, then this is more complete; however, it is not mandatory. If he repented to Allāh without praying and without performing *Wuḍū*, at any time during the night or the day, then indeed Allāh accepts the repentance from his servant, at any time and in any state."[1]

[1] http://www.alfawzan.af.org.sa/node/11418

Glossary

A

Āyah: (pl. āyāt) "sign," a verse of the Qur'ān.
Āhād: a narration which is narrated through one chain only.
Aḥādīth: see ḥadīth.
'Alayhi al-salām: May Allāh (سُبْحَانَهُ وَتَعَالَى) protect and preserve him. It is said after the name of a Prophet of Allāh or after the name of an Angel.
Anṣār: Helpers; the Muslims of al-Madīnah who supported the Muslims who migrated from Makkah.
'Arsh: Throne of Allāh (سُبْحَانَهُ وَتَعَالَى).
'Aṣr: the afternoon Prayer.
Awliyā': see Walī.

B

Bid'ah: Heresy (any innovatory practice).
Burāq: An animal bigger than a donkey and smaller than a horse on which the Prophet (عَلَيْهِ وَعَلَىٰ آلِهِ الصَّلَاةُ وَالسَّلَامُ) went for the Mi'rāj.

D

Dā'ī: One engaged in da'wah, caller.
Ḍa'īf: A weak, unauthentic narration.
Da'wah: Invitation, call to Allāh (سُبْحَانَهُ وَتَعَالَى).
Dīn: a completed way of life prescribed by Allāh (سُبْحَانَهُ وَتَعَالَى).
Dhikr: (pl. adhkār) remembrance of Allāh (جَلَّ جَلَالُهُ) with the heart, sayings of the tongue and actions of our limbs.

F

Fāḥish: One who speaks with evil or obscene speech.

Farḍ Kifāyah: A collective obligation - if fulfilled by a part of the community, then the rest are not obligated.
Fatwā: (pl. fatāwā) A religious verdict.
Faqīh: A Scholar who can give religious verdicts.
Fiqh: Islāmic jurisprudence, understanding.
Fitnah: (pl. fitan) Trials, persecution, conflicts and strifes among the Muslims.
Fitrah: the natural disposition that one is born upon.

G

Ghuluww: Going to an extreme.
Ghusl: A ceremonial bath necessary for the one who is in a state of Janābah (ritual sexual impurity).

H

Ḥadīth: (pl. aḥādīth) the saying, actions and approvals accurately narrated from the Prophet (صَلَّىٰ ٱللَّهُ عَلَيْهِ وَعَلَىٰ آلِهِ وَسَلَّمَ).
Ḥalāl: Lawful.
Ḥanīf: Pure Islāmic Monotheism (worshiping Allāh alone and nothing else).
Ḥarām: Unlawful and forbidden.
Ḥasan: fine, good; a term used for an authentic ḥadīth, which does not reach the level of Ṣaḥīḥ.
Ḥarj: Killing.
Al-Ḥarūriyyah: a special unorthodox religious sect that branched off from the Khawārij.
Hijrah: Migration from the land of Shirk to the land of Islām.
Ḥukm: A judgment of legal decision (especially of Allāh).

I

ʿIbādah: worship, worship of Allāh.
Iḥsān: Worshipping Allāh as though you see Him. However, since you cannot see Him, then know that He sees you.
Ijmāʿ: A consensus, a unified opinion of Scholars regarding a certain issue.

Ijtihād: exertion of effort; the process of arriving at a reasoned decision by a Scholar on an issue.
Imām: A leader; a leader in Prayer, knowledge in fiqh, leader of a state.
Īmān: faith, to affirm all that was revealed to the Prophet (صَلَّىٰ ٱللَّٰهُ عَلَيْهِ وَعَلَىٰ آلِهِ وَسَلَّمَ).
Isnād: the chain of narrators linking the collector of the saying to the person quoted.
Istikhārah: a Prayer consisting of two units (rak'ah) asking Allāh for guidance.
Istiwā: ascending; the ascending of Allāh above the Throne (in the manner that befits His Majesty).

J

Janābah: A state of a person after having sexual intercourse or sexual discharge.
Janāzah: (pl. janaa'iz): Funeral.
Jihād: striving, struggling, fighting to make the Word of Allāh supreme.
Jumu'ah: Friday.
Jinn: invisible creation, created by Allāh from smokeless fire.
Junub: a person who is in the state of janābah.

K

Ka'bah: a square stone building in al-Masjid al-Harām (the great mosque in Makkah which Muslims go to for pilgrimage and to which all Muslims direct their face in Prayer).
Al-Kabā'ir: The major sins.
Khārijī: (pl. Khawārij): Those who declared that a Muslim becomes a disbeliever due to commiting a major sin alone.
Khalīfah: (pl. khulafā'): the head of the Islāmic government to whom the oath of allegiance is given.
Khilāfah: an Islāmic state.
Khuṭbah: (person khaṭīb), religious talk (sermon).
Kufr: (person kāfir) act of disbelief in the Religion of Islām.

M

Madhhab: The position, view or opinion of a Muslim Scholar or school of Islāmic Jurisprudence.
Makrūh: Something that is not approved of, undesirable from the point of view of Religion, although not punishable.
Manhaj: A way; method; methodology.
Marfū': A raised; a narration attributed to the Prophet (صَلَّىٱللَّهُعَلَيْهِوَعَلَىٰٓ آلِهِۦوَسَلَّمَ).
Masjid: A mosque.
Mawbiqāt: great destructive sins.
Mudallis: one who practises tadlīs.
Muhājir: (pl. muhājiroon, muhājirīn) one who migrated from the land of the disbelievers to the land of the Muslims for the sake of Allāh.
Muḥaddith: scholar of the science of ḥadīth.
Muftī: one who gives fatāwā.
Mujāhid: (pl. mujāhidūn): a Muslim warrior in Jihād.
Mujtahid: Someone who is qualified to pass judgment using ijtihād.
Munkar: Rejected; a narration which is inauthentic itself and contradicts and authentic narrations.
Muqallid: one who practices taqlīd.
Mushrik: (pl. mushrikūn) polythesists, pagans and disbelievers in the oneness of Allaah (جَلَّوَعَلَا) and His Messenger (صَلَّىٱللَّهُعَلَيْهِوَسَلَّمَ).
Mustaḥabb: Recommended; an action if left not punishable and if done it is rewardable.
Muttaqūn: People who are pious.
Mutawātir: a ḥadīth which is narrated by a very large number of reporters, such that it cannot be supported that they all agreed upon a lie.
Muwaḥḥid: (pl. muwaḥḥidūn) one who unifies all of his worship and directs it to Allāh alone.
Mawḍū': Fabricated; spurious; invented (narration).
Mawqūf: stopped; a narration from a Companion, which does not go back to the Prophet (صَلَّىٱللَّهُعَلَيْهِوَسَلَّمَ).
Mawṣūl: Connected; a continuous isnād that can be narrated back to the Prophet (صَلَّىٱللَّهُعَلَيْهِوَسَلَّمَ).

N

Nāfilah: (pl. nawāfil) Optional act of worship.
Niyyah: An intention from the heart.
Nusuk: A sacrifice.

Q

Qadar: Divine pre-ordainment; that which Allāh has ordained for His creation.
Qiblah: The direction the Muslims face during Prayer.
Qiyās: Anological deduction of Islāmic laws. New laws are deduced from old laws based upon similarity between their causes.
Qunūt: Devotion; a special supplication while standing in the Prayer.
Quraysh: One of the greatest tribes in Arabia in the pre-Islāmic period of Ignorance. The Prophet (صَلَّى ٱللَّهُ عَلَيْهِ وَسَلَّمَ) belonged to this tribe.

R

Rāfiḍī: This is the correct title for the extreme Shī'ah; those who bear malice and grudges against the noble Companions to the extent that they declare them to be apostates. They also hold that the Qur'ān which the Muslims have is neither complete nor preserved from corruption.
Ramaḍān: The ninth month of Islāmic calander, in which Muslims observe fasting.

S

Ṣaḥābah: Muslims who met the Prophet (صَلَّى ٱللَّهُ عَلَيْهِ وَسَلَّمَ) believing in him and died believing in him.
Ṣaḥīḥ: Authentic, the highest rank of classification of authentic aḥādīth.
Salaf, Salaf al-Ṣāliḥ: The pious predecessors; the Muslims of the first three generations: the Companions, the successors and their successors.
Salafī: one who ascribes oneself to the Salaf and follows their way.
Sīrah: The life story of the Prophet (صَلَّى ٱللَّهُ عَلَيْهِ وَسَلَّمَ).
Sharī'ah: The divine code of law in Islām.
Shawwāl: The month after Ramaḍān.
Shayṭān: Satan.

Shīʿah: (see Rāfiḍī) A collective name for the various sects claiming love for Ahl al-Bayt.
Shirk: Associating partners with Allāh directly or indirectly in worship; compromising any aspects of Tawḥīd.
Sūrah: A chapter of the Qur'ān.
Sunnah: Example, practice; the way of life of the Prophet (صَلَّى ٱللَّهُ عَلَيْهِ وَسَلَّمَ), consisting of his words, actions and silent approvals. The Sunnah is contained in various aḥādīth.

T

Tābiʿī: (pl. tābiʿīn) the generation after the Companions of the Prophet (عَلَيْهِ وَعَلَىٰ آلِهِ ٱلصَّلَاةُ وَٱلسَّلَامُ).
Tafsīr: explanation of the Qur'ān.
Ṭāghūt: Anything that is worshiped other than the real God (Allāh) (i.e. false deities).
Tahajjud: Voluntary, recommended Prayer between the compulsory Prayers of ʿIshā' and Fajr.
Takhrīj: It is to reference a ḥadīth to its sources and analyze its chains of narration.
Taqlīd: Blind following; to follow someone's opinion (madhhab) without evidence.
Taqwā: Acting in obedience to Allāh, hoping for His mercy upon light from Him and taqwā is leaving acts of disobedience, out of fear of Him, upon light from Him.
Tarjamah: Notes about a reporter of ḥadīth.
Ṭawāf: The circumambulation of the kaʿbah.
Tawḥīd: Islāmic Monotheism; the Oneness of Allāh. Believing and acting upon His Lordship, His rights of Worship and Names and Attributes.

U

Uhud: A well known mountain in al-Madīnah. One of the greatest battles in Islāmic history came at its foot. This is called Ghazwah Uhud.
ʿUlamā': (singular: ʿālim) scholars.
Umm: Mother of, used as an identification.

Ummah: Nation, the Muslims as a whole.
'Umrah: A visit to Makkah during which one performs the ṭawāf around the Ka'bah and the Sa'ī between al-Ṣafā and al-Marwah. It is called the lesser Ḥajj.
Uṣūl: The fundamentals.

W

Waḥyī: The revelation or inspiration of Allāh to His Prophets.
Waḥdah al-Wujūd: The belief that everything in existance is intact Allāh. This deviant belief is held by many Ṣūfīyyah.
Wakīl: Disposer of affairs.
Witr: Odd; the last Prayer at the night, which consists of odd number of raka'āt (units).
Walīmah: The wedding feast.
Waṣīlah: the means of approach or achieving His closeness to Allāh by getting His favours.
Wuḍū': An ablution (ritual washing) that is performed before Prayer and other kinds of worship.

Y

Yaqīn: Perfect and absolute faith.
Yathrib: One of the names of al-Madīnah.

Z

Zakāt: Charity that is obligatory on everyone who has wealth over and above a certain limit over which a year has passed (2.5% of saved weath).
Zakāt al-Fiṭr: An obligatory charity by the Muslims to be given to the poor before the Prayer of 'Īd al-Fiṭr.
Zamzam: The sacred water inside the ḥaram (the grand mosque) at Makkah.
Zanādiqah: An atheist, a heretic.

Our Call to the Ummah

[1]: We believe in Allāh and His Names and Attributes, as they were mentioned in the Book of Allāh and in the *Sunnah* of the Messenger of Allāh (عَزَّوَجَلَّ), without *taḥrīf* (distortion), nor *ta'wīl* (figurative interpretation), nor *tamthīl* (making a likeness), nor *tashbīh* (resemblance), nor *ta'ṭīl* (denial).

[2]: We love the Companions (رَضِيَٱللَّهُعَنْهُمْ) of the Messenger of Allaah (صَلَّىٱللَّهُعَلَيْهِوَسَلَّمَ), and we hate those who speak against them. We believe that to speak ill of them is to speak ill of the Religion, because they are the ones who conveyed it to us. And we love the Family of the Prophet (صَلَّىٱللَّهُعَلَيْهِوَسَلَّمَ) with love that is permitted by the *Sharī'ah*. 'Imrān Ibn Ḥusayn (رَضِيَٱللَّهُعَنْهُ) said, "O people! Learn the knowledge of the Religion from us, if you do not do so, then you will certainly be misguided."[1]

[3]: We love the People of *Ḥadīth* and all of the *Salaf* of the *Ummah* from *Ahl al-Sunnah*. Imām al-Shāṭibī (d.790H) - رَحِمَهُٱللَّهُ - said, "The *Salaf al-Ṣāliḥ*, the Companions, the *tābi'īn* and their successors knew the *Qur'ān*, its sciences and its meanings the best."[2]

[4]: We despise *'ilm al-kalām* (knowledge of theological rhetoric), and we view it to be from amongst the greatest reasons for the division in the *Ummah*.

[5]: We do not accept anything from the books of *fiqh* (jurisprudence), nor from the books of *tafsīr* (explanation of the *Qur'ān*), nor from the ancient stories, nor from the *Sīrah* (biography) of the Prophet (صَلَّىٱللَّهُعَلَيْهِوَسَلَّمَ), except that which has been confirmed from Allāh or from His Messenger (صَلَّىٱللَّهُعَلَيْهِوَسَلَّمَ). We do not mean that we have rejected them, nor do we claim that we are not in need of them. Rather, we benefit from the discoveries

[1] Refer to *al-Kifāyah* (p. 15) of al-Khaṭīb al-Baghdādī.
[2] Refer to *al-Muwāfiqāt* (2/79) of al-Shāṭibī.

of our Scholars and the jurists and other than them. However, we do not accept a ruling, except with an authentic proof.

[6]: We do not write in our books, nor do we cover in our lessons, nor do we give sermons with anything except the *Qur'ān*, or the authentic and authoritative *ḥadīth*. And we detest what emanates from many books and admonishers in terms of false stories and weak and fabricated *aḥādīth*. ʿAbdullāh Ibn al-Mubārak (d.181H) - رَحِمَهُ ٱللَّهُ - said, "The authentic *aḥādīth* are sufficient and the weak *aḥādīth* are not needed."[1]

[7]: We do not perform *takfīr* upon any Muslim due to any sin, except *Shirk* with Allāh, or the abandonment of Prayer, or apostasy. We seek refuge in Allāh from that.

[8]: We believe that the *Qur'ān* is the Speech of Allāh, it is not created.

[9]: We hold that our 'obligation is to co-operate with the group that traverses the methodology of the Book and the *Sunnah*, and what the *Salaf* of the *Ummah* were upon; in terms of calling to Allāh (سُبْحَانَهُ وَتَعَالَىٰ), and being sincere in worship of Him, and warning from *Shirk*, innovations, and disobedience, and to advise all of the groups that oppose this.'[2] 'So co-operating upon righteousness and piety (*taqwā*) and mutual advising necessitates warning against evil and not co-operating with the wicked.'[3]

[10]: We do not deem it correct to revolt against the Muslim rulers as long as they are Muslims, nor do we feel that revolutions bring about reconciliation. Rather, they corrupt the community.

---

[1] Refer to *al-Jāmiʿ li-Akhlāq al-Rāwī* (2/159) of al-Suyūṭī.

[2] From a *fatwā* by the Committee of Major Scholars dated: 11/16/1417H, (no. 18870). It was signed by al-ʿAllāmah ʿAbd al-ʿAzīz Ibn Bāz, Shaykh ʿAbd al-ʿAzīz Ibn ʿAbdullāh Āl al-Shaykh, Shaykh ʿAbdullāh Ibn ʿAbd al-Raḥmān al-Ghudayyān, Shaykh Bakr Ibn ʿAbdullāh Abū Zayd, and Shaykh Ṣāliḥ Ibn Fawzān al-Fawzān.

[3] From the words of Shaykh Ibn Bāz in *al-Furqān* magazine (issue no. 14, p. 15).

[11]: We hold that this multiplicity of present day parties is a reason for the division of the Muslims and their weakness. So therefore we set about 'freeing the minds from the fetters of blind-following and the darkness of sectarianism and party spirit.'[1]

[12]: We restrict our understanding of the Book of Allāh and of the *Sunnah* of the Messenger of Allāh (صَلَّىٰ ٱللَّٰهُ عَلَيْهِ وَسَلَّمَ) to the understanding of the *Salaf* of the *Ummah* from the Scholars of *ḥadīth*, not the blind-followers of their individuals. Rather, we take the truth from wherever it comes. And we know that there are those who claim *Salafiyyah*, yet *Salafiyyah* is free from them, since they bring to the society what Allāh has prohibited. We believe in 'cultivating the young generation upon this Islām, purified from all that we have mentioned, giving to them a correct Islāmic education from the start - without any influence from the disbelieving western education.'[2]

[13]: We believe that politics is a part of the Religion, and those who try to separate the Religion from politics are only attempting to destroy the Religion and to spread chaos.

[14]: We believe there will be no honour or victory for the Muslims until they return to the Book of Allaah and to the *Sunnah* of the Messenger of Allāh (صَلَّىٰ ٱللَّٰهُ عَلَيْهِ وَسَلَّمَ).

[15]: We oppose those who divide the Religion into trivialities and important issues. And we know that this is a destructive *da'wah.*

[16]: We oppose those who put down the knowledge of the *Sunnah*, and say that this is not the time for it. Likewise, we oppose those who put down acting upon the *Sunnah* of the Messenger of Allāh (صَلَّىٰ ٱللَّٰهُ عَلَيْهِ وَسَلَّمَ).

---

[1] From *Fiqh al-Wāqi'* (p. 49) of al-Albānī.

[2] From *Fiqh al-Waaqi'* (p. 51) of al-Albānī.

[17]: Our *da'wah* and our *'aqīdah* is more beloved to us than our own selves, our wealth and our offspring. So we are not prepared to part with it for gold, nor silver. We say this so that no one may have hope in buying out our *da'wah*, nor should he think that it is possible for him to purchase it from us for *dīnār* or *dirham*.

[18]: We love the present day Scholars of the *Sunnah* and hope to benefit from them and regret the passing away of many of them. Imām Mālik said (d.179H) - رَحِمَهُ ٱللَّهُ, "The knowledge of *ḥadīth* is your flesh and blood and you will be asked concerning it on the Day of Judgement, so look who you are taking it from."[1]

[19]: We do not accept a *fatwā* except from the Book of Allāh and the *Sunnah* of the Messenger of Allāh (صَلَّى ٱللَّهُ عَلَيْهِ وَسَلَّمَ).

These are glimpses into our *'aqīdah* and our *da'wah*. So if one has any objection to this, then we are prepared to accept advice if it is truthful, and to refute it if it is erroneous, and to avoid it if it is stubborn rejection. And Allāh knows best.

---

[1] Refer to *al-Muḥaddith al-Fāṣil* (p. 416) and *al-Kifāyah* (p. 21) of al-Khaṭīb.